Library of
Davidson College

Collective Bargaining in the Railroad Industry

Collective Bargaining in the Railroad Industry

JACOB J. KAUFMAN

NEW YORK / RUSSELL & RUSSELL

COPYRIGHT, 1952, BY JACOB J. KAUFMAN
FIRST PUBLISHED IN BOOK FORM, 1954
REISSUED, 1973, BY RUSSELL & RUSSELL
A DIVISION OF ATHENEUM PUBLISHERS, INC.
BY ARRANGEMENT WITH JACOB J. KAUFMAN
L. C. CATALOG CARD NO: 72-84992
ISBN 0-8462-1694-9
PRINTED IN THE UNITED STATES OF AMERICA

To T. G.

PREFACE

THE WRITER has participated in hearings before emergency and arbitration boards established in accordance with the provisions of the Railway Labor Act, as amended. Out of this experience have come three observations with respect to labor relations in the railroad industry: first, the collective bargaining relationships are unusually complex; second, the popular belief that collective bargaining relationships have been mature and responsible is erroneous; third, in the past decade a number of serious strikes or threatened strikes have occurred. The last two observations naturally called for an explanation. The first observation made the answer only more difficult.

For assisting me in arriving at an understanding of many of the complexities in the labor relations in the railroad industry I want to express my appreciation to officials of the railroad labor organizations, the railroad industry, and the government. I am indebted to Professor Paul F. Brissenden of the Graduate School of Business, Columbia University, for reading the preliminary drafts of the manuscript with great care and making many helpful suggestions. Professors Eli Ginzberg and Ernest W. Williams, Jr., of the same faculty, have also been kind enough to read the manuscript and offer pertinent suggestions.

I am particularly indebted to two persons who have had considerable influence in the writing of the book. One is the late Professor John D. Sumner of the Department of Economics, the University of Buffalo. The other person is one who shall simply be referred to as "the Boss." My debt to these two is great and indescribable. Finally, I should like to refer to the various members of the Department of Economics of the University of Buffalo who unknowingly have assisted me in many ways. None of these persons, of course, is in any way responsible for any errors in the book of any sort, but each has helped considerably in minimizing their number.

The *Southern Economic Journal* has been kind enough to permit me to reprint my article, "Grievance Procedures Under the Railway Labor Act," as Chapter XI.

JACOB J. KAUFMAN

July, 1953
Buffalo, New York

CONTENTS

I. INTRODUCTION   1

PART I: BACKGROUND

II. THE RAILROAD INDUSTRY   4
III. EMPLOYMENT, METHODS OF WAGE PAYMENT, AND WORKING RULES   18
IV. THE LABOR ORGANIZATIONS   45
V. FEDERAL INTERVENTION IN RAILWAY LABOR DISPUTES   55

PART II: THE RAILWAY LABOR ACT IN OPERATION

VI. THE RAILWAY LABOR ACT: SUCCESS OR FAILURE?   74
VII. THE RECORD: 1934–1952   78
VIII. THE EARNINGS POSITION OF RAILROAD WORKERS   90
IX. WAGE STANDARDS OF EMERGENCY BOARDS   95
X. COMPULSION IN THE SETTLEMENT OF RAILWAY LABOR DISPUTES   127
XI. BREAKDOWN OF GRIEVANCE PROCEDURES   137
XII. DEFECTS IN THE RAILWAY LABOR ACT   153

PART III: STRIKES AFFECTING THE PUBLIC INTEREST

XIII. THE RIGHT OF RAILROAD WORKERS TO STRIKE 162

PART IV: CONCLUSION

XIV. SUMMARY AND RECOMMENDATIONS 179
NOTES 187
BIBLIOGRAPHY 217
INDEX 231

LIST OF TABLES

1. Distribution of Railroad Workers by Occupational Groups, 1939 and December 1952   20
2. Work Stoppages in the Railroad Industry, 1934–1949   79
3. Average Hourly Earnings, Workers in Manufacturing Industries and the Railroad Industry, 1936–1952   91

CHAPTER I

INTRODUCTION

ALFRED MARSHALL has said that "the dominant economic fact of our own age is the development not of the manufacturing, but of the transport industries."[1] The transportation industry—which includes railroads, trucks, inland waterways, oil pipe lines, and air carriers—has permitted the peoples of the world to achieve a greater output of goods and services with a given amount of resources. Even more, it has permitted the peoples of the world to utilize certain resources which otherwise would very likely not have been available for use. And the American railroads, which handle somewhat less than two thirds of the total freight traffic and more than one half of the total passenger traffic in the United States, played, and continue to play, a major role in American economic development.[2]

The significant role of the railroad industry in American economic life cannot be measured in terms of the actual value of its services directly produced. Rather the contribution of the railroad industry to the American standard of living would be measured best if we were able to withdraw its facilities from the economy and then measure the net reduction in the gross national product. Such an impossible experiment would quickly reveal the extent to which the railroad industry, by attacking the obstacle of physical separation, "enables a given flow of resources to produce greater results."[3]

The recent strikes or threatened strikes in the railroad industry have given us a glimpse of what would happen if the railroad industry were completely closed down. The transfer of the products of farms and factories, as well as the movement of peoples from point to point, began to grind slowly to a halt. Were it not for goods in inventory the entire economy would have been paralyzed. And no air lift, such as was employed in Germany, could meet the needs of the American economy.

As a result of strikes or threatened strikes, both during the years of World War II and the postwar period, the President of the United States has ordered the seizure of most of the nation's railroads four times and in other instances has ordered the seizure of individual railroads, the closing down of which, in his opinion, threatened the welfare of the economy.

The problem of strikes on the nation's railroads has been particularly acute during the postwar years and there has been increasing public concern over this question. In view of the fact that the Railway Labor Act, as amended, provides for certain procedures to be followed when labor disputes arise in the railroad industry, and has been described as a "model labor law" by governmental leaders and students of labor relations, the following questions naturally arise:

1. What has caused the increasing number, as well as extent, of strikes and threatened strikes in the railroad industry?
2. What improvements may be made either in the law itself or the procedures governing labor relations in the industry in order to reduce the number, as well as the extent, of these strikes?
3. Should strikes be permitted in the railroad industry as a matter of public policy?
4. What are the implications of the prohibition of strikes in the railroad industry?

The writer in the course of the discussion will attempt to answer these questions.

In Part I the importance of the railroad industry to the economy is discussed. In addition, the impact of the financial

INTRODUCTION 3

condition and the increasing mechanization of the industry upon the employment and working conditions of the railroad workers is analyzed. Finally, a description of the labor organizations and a history of governmental intervention in railway labor disputes are presented. Part II is concerned chiefly with the causes of the breakdown of the Railway Labor Act in settling labor disputes. Part III consists of a discussion of the pros and cons of withholding from the railroad workers the right to strike and considers the implications of such public policy. Part IV sets forth conclusions and recommendations.

The Railway Labor Act, as amended, is concerned with four aspects of industrial relations in the railroad industry: (1) the settlement of labor disputes arising out of contract negotiations or changes and involving such procedures as mediation, voluntary arbitration, and emergency boards;[4] (2) the arbitration or adjudication of labor disputes arising out of interpretation and application of collective bargaining contracts —the grievance disputes handled by the National Railroad Adjustment Board; (3) the prevention of unfair labor practices on the part of railroad managers; and (4) the determination of employee representation. This study is concerned, primarily, with the first two of these.[5]

Part I: Background

CHAPTER II

THE RAILROAD INDUSTRY

IT IS the purpose of this chapter to provide a general background of the railroad industry. First, there is presented information on the size and importance of the industry, indicating not only the extent to which the traffic in the industry is concentrated in the hands of a relatively small number of railroads but also the potential effect of a railroad strike on the economy. Second, the financial condition of the railroads is discussed in order to indicate its effect on the labor relations in the industry. Third, the technological advances made in the industry, particularly in recent years, are analyzed for the purpose of pointing to their impact on employment and the collective bargaining relationships.

SIZE AND IMPORTANCE

The railroad industry in 1952 had nearly $26 billion invested in property in order to handle over 600 billion ton-miles of freight traffic, including goods of the farms, mines, forests, and factories, and about 34 billion passenger-miles of passenger traffic over a network of about 225,000 miles of railway line.[1] In order to meet the demand for these services the industry employed during 1952 on the average more than 1,200,000 workers and paid them nearly $5,300,000,000 in the form of wages and salaries for working over 2.8 billion hours.[2]

The railroad system reaches into every state, and a map showing the distribution of railway mileage indicates that every important city in the continental United States has a railroad. As is to be expected, there is a great density of mileage in the eastern and midwestern states as contrasted with the western states, reflecting the degree of industrialization of these areas. The South also has a wide network of railway mileage because of the need for the transportation of farm products.[3]

A large amount of freight and passenger traffic funnels through a few central points and is carried by a relatively small number of the larger railways. A map of the major rail routes in the United States shows that such cities as New York, Buffalo, Chicago, St. Louis, Kansas City, St. Paul–Minneapolis, and Birmingham are important railroad junctions where the major railroad lines converge.

The Interstate Commerce Commission classifies railroads into three groups: Class I railroads include those whose operating revenues are greater than $1,000,000 per year; Class II railroads have operating revenues of between $100,000 and $1,000,000; and Class III railroads are those with operating revenues of less than $100,000. Of 464 such railroads in the three groups, there were, at the beginning of 1951, 127 in the Class I category.[4]

This group of 127 railroads handles about 95 percent of the tons of freight originated by the railroads and over 99 percent of the passengers carried by all of the railroads.[5] But twenty-five of the larger railroads handled about two thirds of the revenue freight tonnage of the Class I railroads.[6]

The small number of important railroad terminals through which the major railroad systems pass and the small number of railroads which carry the major part of the freight tonnage offer the labor organizations in the industry an opportunity to obtain strategic control over the railroad system in a limited number of areas and on a limited number of railroads.

This strategic control was referred to in the decision of the District Court in Buffalo when the Switchmen's Union of North America (AF of L) was enjoined from striking against a single railroad—the Chicago, Rock Island, and Pacific—

because such a strike, in the words of the judge, deprives "the nation of an essential transportation service and will substantially obstruct the flow of interstate commerce and the transmission of the mails of the United States over the affected railway system." [7] It should be noted that the Court also pointed out that the union represented only a small portion of the workers of the railroad but was in a peculiarly strategic position to halt the operations of the railroad.[8]

A railroad official has stated that "the effects of a strike on a major railroad are not confined" to the plants and industries directly connected with the railroad, but "spread out literally over the whole Nation." He pointed out, for example, that 67 percent of the freight handled by the Pennsylvania Railroad either originates on, or is finally delivered by, another railroad, and that "the economic effects of a stoppage of transportation would inevitably spread out everywhere through the national economy." [9] The effects of a strike on other large railroads are similar in nature.

Financial Condition

Besides the vulnerability of the railroad industry to strikes because of the concentration of traffic on a relatively small number of railroads and at a few terminals, one finds that the industry is beset with a financial problem, the nature of which is described below. The question arises as to the extent to which the financial position of the railroads has forced them to resist the demands of their employees and to utilize the procedures of the Railway Labor Act, as amended, rather than deal with their employees on the basis of direct negotiations. To answer this question, it is necessary, first, to describe briefly the financial condition of the railroad industry; second, to explain the economic factors involved; and third, to examine some of the rate-setting procedures which may affect the ability of the railroads to meet the demands of their employees by direct negotiation.

THE RATE OF RETURN

In the determination of the adequacy of the profits of the railroad industry—for that matter, of any industry—the first question to be answered is what standard or standards should be employed. It has been suggested that the Supreme Court has set forth the standards succinctly in *Bluefield Waterworks Co. v. Public Service Commission,* 262 U. S. 679 (1923), when it said that "the return should be reasonably sufficient to assure confidence in the financial soundness of the utility and should be adequate, under efficient and economical management, to maintain and support its credit and enable it to raise the money necessary for the proper discharge of its public duties." [10]

A variety of measures has been employed by the railroads to indicate that their earnings have been inadequate in order "to provide the safe, adequate, economical and efficient transportation service contemplated by the National Transportation Policy and upon which service the welfare of our nation so greatly depends, not only in time of war, but also in time of peace." [11] The railroads point out, first, that their return on net assets—that is, the ratio of net income to net assets (by net assets is meant "the sum of the book value of outstanding preferred and common stock plus the surplus account at the beginning of the year, and excludes all indebtedness")—is considerably lower than the average return for manufacturing corporations and for other publicly regulated utilities.[12] Second, the railroads attempt to show that their earnings are inadequate by comparing their actual rate of return on net investment with a standard figure of 5.9 percent which the Interstate Commerce Commission once indicated was what the railroads should earn in a "constructive normal year." [13]

The actual rates of return on net investment for the past thirteen years have been as follows: [14]

Year	Percent
1940	2.94
1941	4.28
1942	6.34
1943	5.75
1944	4.73
1945	3.77
1946	2.75
1947	3.41
1948	4.24
1949	2.86
1950	4.22
1951	3.69
1952	4.00

According to the railroads these rates of return on net investment are inadequate to meet all fixed charges; "to provide compensation for the owners of equity capital"; "to attract necessary capital funds into the industry"; "to enable the accumulation of surpluses to meet possible contingencies and otherwise to maintain the credit standing of the carriers"; and to provide adequate compensation to management.[15] The inadequacy of these rates of return to meet these objectives has been described in a recent study published by The Brookings Institution.[16]

To what can the inadequate earnings of the railroads be attributed? There are three basic causes: The increasing competition of other forms of transportation has resulted in a decline in the railroads' proportion of intercity freight traffic; the inadequacies in the rate-making procedures have seriously affected the railroads' financial position; and finally, the opposition of labor to the consolidation of railroads and the ineffective power of the Interstate Commerce Commission have, in large measure, prevented the railroads from improving their financial position. Each of these three points will be discussed in turn.

COMPETITION AND THE RAILROADS

The distribution of commercial intercity freight traffic and passenger traffic in the United States indicates that the proportion handled by the railroads, as compared with other forms of transportation such as rivers and canals, motor trucks, oil pipe lines, electric railroads, and air carriers, declined prior to the outbreak of World War II, rose after the outbreak of the war, and after reaching a peak in 1943, declined again.[17] This decline in the proportion of traffic handled by the railroads can be ascribed, for the most part, to the fact that "some forms of transportation enjoy the free, or partially free, use of publicly financed facilities" while "others [including the railroads] must finance their entire plant from operating revenues." [18]

A second factor which has placed the railroads in a relatively poor position competitively has been the "universal obligation" which the railroads have to carry freight and passengers, while "private and exempt carriers . . . can pick and choose the traffic which they will handle." [19] This specialized competition is also found in the case of certain common carriers, such as water and motor transportation, since these agencies of transportation often "confine their operations to principal points where there is an assured volume of desirable transportation." [20]

RATE-MAKING PROCEDURES

The relatively poor earnings of the railroads, it is also asserted, reflect certain inadequacies both in the rate-making process in the railroad industry, as well as in the public policy of control. One problem has been that the Interstate Commerce Commission "has consistently reserved the right to substitute its business judgment for that of railroad management."[21] As a result, the railroads' judgment as to rate changes, based on economic considerations, has been frequently rejected. It has also been suggested that procedural delays in the approval of rates by the Commission have had certain serious short-run financial consequences.[22] As a result of such delays—in the form of long, drawn-out proceedings—the railroads do not have an opportunity to put into effect increased rates until the Commission approves them. The new rates are not made retroactive, while the increased wage rates agreed upon by the railroad labor organizations and the carriers are usually made retroactive.[23] In view of the fact that the wage bill of the railroads represents nearly one half of their total operating expenses, significant wage increases may have a substantial effect upon the financial condition of the railroads.[24]

It has been suggested, further, that railroad rates have not kept pace with the general price changes during the past decade and this "rigidity of railroad rates" is explained by the fact that "the price of railroad service is rigidly controlled by public authority, while other industries are free to adjust price to current demand."[25] From 1942 to 1952 the revenue per ton-mile increased from 0.932 cents to 1.410 cents, or 51 percent, and the revenue per passenger-mile increased from 1.916 cents to 2.600 cents, or 36 percent.[26] This compares with an increase in the index of wholesale prices of about 80 percent during the same period.[27] This increase in prices of other goods and services considered in conjunction with the increase in average hourly earnings of 154 percent during the same period would seem to indicate a severe squeeze on the railroads.[28] However, one must take into account several factors which would tend to reduce this apparent severe impact on the finances of the railroads.[29] First, during this period the output per man hour increased nearly 60 percent, reflecting in part the large increase in the volume of freight traffic with a much smaller increase in the number of workers employed to meet this increased demand for railroad service. Secondly, the railroads operate under decreasing costs and the increased freight activity was not accompanied by corresponding increases in costs. Finally, during this period the Interstate Commerce Commission had authorized increases in railroad freight rates amounting to 79 percent, although the revenue per ton-mile has risen only 43 percent.[30] The explanation for this discrepancy lies in the fact that the railroads have not been able to exploit fully the rate increases granted by the Commission because of the competitive situation which the railroads face and the "changes in the composition of traffic and in length of hauls for particular commodities." [31]

All of these "easing" factors were not sufficient to offset the rise in prices that the railroads have faced, with the result that unit costs have risen more than average revenue. Thus, the profit per unit of traffic has fallen. The rise in traffic volume, however, has resulted in an increase in total profits.[32] This increase, according to the railroads and as indicated above, is still insufficient to yield an adequate return compared to other industries.

The effect of the Commission's control over rate increases becomes more evident during periods of great economic activity. With the demand for transportation services relatively inelastic during periods of war or active defense, the railroads would, if permitted, have an opportunity to increase their revenues by raising rates without too serious concern about the competitive situation. Such increased revenues might provide substantial reserves for future investments. But the Commission has usually resisted significant rate increases during periods of great economic activity. During World War II, for example, the authorization of a rate increase of 4.7 percent (on the average) of March 18, 1942, was suspended effective May 15, 1943, when railroad traffic was unusually heavy. Thus, during the entire period of the war no general change in rates was authorized by the Commission. It was not until July 1, 1946, that any general rate change was allowed. Similarly, in 1951 a 6 to 9 percent increase in rates was allowed by the Commission (the railroads asked for a 15 percent increase), but the authority for the higher rates expired on February 28, 1953.[33] On April 11, 1952, the railroads were granted the full 15 percent, and the I.C.C. reserved the right to re-examine its action any time prior to February 28, 1953.[34] Apparently, the failure to permit the railroads to adjust quickly to changes in operating expenses and to raise their rates during periods of high business activity prevents the railroads from realizing "a sufficiently high level of earnings . . . to tide them over recurring traffic and profit famines." [35]

CONSOLIDATION OF RAILROADS

It would seem that during "normal" periods of business activity the problem is not necessarily one of rigid public control, but rather one of competition. How can the railroads improve their financial situation during such years? It has been suggested that one way would be a more aggressive policy of consolidation on the part of the Commission.[36] Such consolidation would eliminate duplicate lines and services, and unify and improve terminal facilities in the major railroad centers.[37] Apparently, the present powers of the Commission are either ineffective or insufficient.[38] Furthermore, any widespread consolidation program has usually encountered strong opposition from the railroad labor organizations, since the effect of consolidation would be a reduction in employment in the railroad industry.[39] The Interstate Commerce Act provides that the Commission, in passing upon any plan for consolidation, shall consider (among other things) "the interest of the carrier employees affected" and "shall require a fair and equitable arrangement to protect the interests of the railroad employees affected." [40] The law provides further that "in its order of approval, the Commission shall include terms and conditions providing that during the period of four years from the effective date" of any consolidation order "such transaction will not result in employees of the carrier or carriers by railroad affected by such order being in a worse position with respect to their employment, except that the protection afforded to any employee pursuant to this sentence shall not be required to continue for a longer period, following the effective date of such order, than the period during which such employee was in the employ of such carrier or carriers prior to the effective date of such order." [41] The law also permits the employees and the carriers to enter into any agreement "pertaining to the protection of the interests" of the employees.[42] These provisions were originally included in the Emergency Railroad Transportation Act of June 16, 1933, but since this act was intended as an emergency measure, the railroad labor organizations entered into an agreement with the carriers along the same lines (the substance of which was included in the Interstate Commerce Act, revised by the Transportation Act of 1940 and quoted above), an agreement commonly referred to as the "Washington Job Protection Agreement." [43] Under the agreement railroad workers who are retained after the consolidation are guaranteed that, for a period of not more than five years, they will either retain their jobs or be transferred to other jobs with equal pay and similar working conditions. The number of years for which the assurance is given depends upon the number of years the workers have been employed, but in no case can exceed five years. Those workers whose services are terminated receive an allowance based on their length of service. Payments may be made in the form of monthly payments, or "lump sum" allowances.[44]

Apparently the labor organizations have applied pressure upon the Interstate Commerce Commission in cases involving consolidations, and in those instances where they have failed to block consolidations, they have been able to apply the provisions of the agreement.[45] Thus, a significant—if not crucial—method by which the financial position of the railroads might be improved is hindered by the interests of the railroad labor organizations, who see that consolidations represent not only a threat to employment, but also to the union organization itself. It might be suggested that the I.C.C.'s present ineffective policy with respect to consolidations also reflects the political pressures of the railroad labor organizations.

Thus, on the one hand, when the railroads have an opportunity to improve their financial position during periods of prosperity, they find themselves unable to increase their rates as much as they would desire because of the control by the Interstate Commerce Commission. On the other hand, during "normal" periods, or periods of depression, when consolidation might be desirable (either voluntarily or by compulsion), the railroad labor organizations strongly resist such a program. This resistance to consolidation would also prevail during periods of great economic activity but not to the same extent. In fact, during the present period of high employment it might be desirable to push more strongly for consolidation so that the employment effects would be minimized.

In conclusion, it is suggested that the opposition of the railroads to the wage demands of the railroad labor organizations and the failure of the railroads to bargain "on the property" stem, in part, from the inadequate earning power of the railroads. This inadequate earning power reflects, on the one hand, the restrictive policy of the Interstate Commerce Commisison with respect to increased rates during periods of prosperity. With a restrictive policy in effect during such periods it is suggested that, if the railroads would want to be compensated (in the form of rate increases) for any increases in their wage costs, the railroads would not agree "on the property" to wage increases, but would resist such demands and oppose them before emergency boards so that they would have a better case before the Commission. If the railroads would voluntarily agree to such demands their case before the Commission might be seriously affected. On the other hand, during so-called "normal" periods, when the solution to the railroads' financial position lies more in the area of reducing expenses—say, by consolidation of roads and facilities—rather than in rate increases (because of the competitive situation), the railroads face the opposition of the railroad labor organizations who fear the employment effects and the threat to the labor organizations themselves.

Thus, the financial and competitive condition of the railroads and the rate-making procedures of the Interstate Commerce Commission seriously affect the collective bargaining relationships between the carriers and their employees and explain, in part, the recurring strikes and the breakdown of collective bargaining in the industry.

Technological Changes

For many years the railroads have made "changes in roadbed, rails, rolling stock, and methods of operation" in a search for economies in operation that would provide greater safety and would help to meet competition.[46] As a result of such changes, employment in the industry, during the twenty years prior to 1939, dropped by about 40 percent.[47] With the outbreak of the war in 1939, this downward trend in employment was reversed, but at the close of the war employment again began to fall.[48]

In recent years, particularly since the end of World War II, the railroads have carried on an extensive mechanization program, both on the roads and in the yards. It was not until the thirties that the railroads began to realize the full implications of competition from other sources of transportation, but they lacked the financial resources with which to improve their plant. During World War II, when these financial resources were available, the railroads had difficulty in obtaining equipment. But after the war, faced with the growing competition of other forms of transportation, the railroads embarked on a mechanization and dieselization program. It is the rapid dieselization and the increased mechanization of the railroads in recent years which may explain the growing militancy of the employees and their labor organizations, who view this process as a threat. To meet this threat the workers have sought, and continue to seek, ways and means of stabilizing their employment.[49]

The dieselization of the railroads in recent years is indicated by the fact that in 1939 only 510 locomotives out of a total of 42,511 locomotives in service were of the diesel-electric type; near the end of 1952 over 15,000 diesel-electric units were in service out of a total of over 31,000.[50] In other words, the diesel locomotive today represents nearly one half of the total number of locomotives in service. The potential savings in the use of a diesel are revealed by the fact that this type of locomotive requires very little servicing and therefore can be utilized nearly eighteen hours a day in the yard; the average steam locomotive can be used about eight hours a day.[51] Another indication of the potential savings from the use of a diesel is the low fuel cost. The fuel cost per unit of traffic for a diesel is about two-thirds to one-half less than that for a steam locomotive, depending upon the type of service for which the engine is employed.[52] An attempt has been made to estimate the potential savings to the railroads in the year 1948 from the displacement of steam by diesel power, assuming 1948 unit costs and based on the 1946–1949 level of operation. Such potential savings were estimated to be more than one billion dollars.[53]

In addition to the dieselization program, the railroads have, since the end of World War II, purchased large quantities of maintenance machinery, and installed large quantities of materials-handling equipment, communications equipment, signaling devices, power switches, and car-retarders.[54] This mechanization program has been accelerated in recent years and is designed to reduce costs of operation through savings in man-hours of work.[55] It is estimated, for example, that in 1952 the railroads spent approximately $1.3 billion for new equipment and fixed facilities.[56]

Conclusion

The railroad industry is "big business." Confronted on the one hand by the Interstate Commerce Commission, which prevents it from obtaining additional revenue during periods of great economic activity, and on the other hand by increasing competition and greater wage demands from its employees, the industry has turned to technology in order to reduce its costs of operation. This means that the workers on the railroads are threatened by the loss of their jobs and the labor organizations are confronted with a loss of power. These conditions are at the bottom of the conflict between the carriers and their employees. The impact of these technological changes on employment and the devices employed by the workers in an attempt to offset their displacement are discussed in the next chapter.

CHAPTER III

EMPLOYMENT, METHODS OF WAGE PAYMENT, AND WORKING RULES

A STUDY of the employment, the methods of wage payment, and working rules of the railroad workers reveals three outstanding facts: first, prior to World War II and after 1945 employment in the industry steadily declined; second, the methods of wage payment for the so-called road men are unique; and third, the rules covering the work of most of the operating men and some of the nonoperating workers are unusually complex. These facts are presented not for descriptive purposes, but primarily to indicate the extent to which they contribute to the difficulties under which collective bargaining is carried on and which are encountered in the operations of the Railway Labor Act.

EMPLOYMENT

From 1921 to 1939, employment on the steam railroads in the United States dropped by about 40 percent as contrasted with a drop in manufacturing employment of slightly less than 10 percent.[1] From 1939 to 1945 employment on the railroads increased from nearly 970,000 to over 1,460,000.[2] From this peak, employment again fell to slightly more than 1,240,000 in June, 1950.[3] After this month, with the outbreak of the Korean War, employment rose slightly in 1951, and then declined in 1952, so that during December 1952 about 1,200,000 workers were employed.[4]

Accompanying this long-run decline in employment has been the phenomenon of cyclical fluctuation in employment accompanying cyclical fluctuations in traffic, although the changes in employment—in either direction—do not tend to be as great as the changes in traffic.[5]

While railroad employment declined about 40 percent from 1921 to 1939, the tons of freight carried one mile increased by about 10 percent, and passenger traffic decreased by about 40 percent.[6] Passenger traffic, however, accounted for only 11 percent of the total traffic revenue in 1939.[7] From 1939 to 1945, employment on the railroads, as mentioned previously, increased by about 50 percent, while freight traffic more than doubled and passenger traffic increased more than fourfold.[8] Since the peak employment in 1945, railroad employment has fallen by about 14 percent (as of December, 1952) while freight traffic in 1952 was approximately 10 percent below that for 1945.[9] Passenger traffic, during 1952, however, was about 63 percent below the 1945 peak.[10]

These data indicate that over the past three decades and during the postwar years (1946 to 1952) the output per worker has been increasing significantly. During the years prior to the war the significant factors contributing to greater output have been heavier carloads, more cars per train, higher speeds of trains, and greater utilization of equipment.[11] Basic to this increased output was the ability of locomotives to pull heavier and larger loads. Prior to 1939 the locomotives were either made larger or other technical improvements were made.[12] Since the war, as indicated in the preceding chapter, the "diesel revolution" has not only brought about increased output but also some displacement of labor.[13]

The prewar decline in railroad employment and the failure of employment to keep pace with increased railroad activity during and after the war, have been disturbing elements in the collective bargaining relationships in the railroad industry. It is true that between 1939 and 1952, the number of workers employed rose from 970,000 to 1,226,000, or about 26 percent.[14] But during the same period freight traffic increased about 84 percent, while passenger traffic increased by about 51 percent.[15] Yet, despite the increase in total employment, in many types of work, particularly among the road operating workers, the number of employed decreased, remained roughly the same, or increased only slightly, as can be observed in Table 1.[16] As a result, the unions demanded that certain rules be imposed which would maintain employment and the strength of the road operating unions as well. The disparity between the change in employment and the increase in railroad activity has also been an impetus to strong demands for wage increases. Regardless of the merits of the controversy, it has given the workers an impression that they have not shared in the benefits of the increased technology of the industry.[17]

TABLE 1

DISTRIBUTION OF RAILROAD WORKERS BY OCCUPATIONAL GROUPS, 1939 AND DECEMBER, 1952

Type of Work	1939	December 1952
Executives, officials, and staff assistants	11,745	15,876
Professional, clerical and general	163,056	208,895
Maintenance of way and structures	201,943	232,621
Maintenance of equipment and stores	264,160	347,994
Transportation (other than train, engine, and yard)	125,149	145,084
Transportation (yardmasters, switch tenders and hostlers)	12,141	15,791
Transportation (train and engine)	209,749	256,469
Road passenger conductors	6,893	6,604
Assistant road passenger conductors and ticket collectors	1,143	2,796
Road freight conductors (through)	8,899	10,840
Road freight conductors (local and way)	6,186	6,849
Road passenger baggagemen	3,853	3,774
Road passenger brakemen and flagmen	9,094	8,397

EMPLOYMENT

Type of Work	1939	December 1952
Road freight brakemen and flagmen (through)	23,087	26,771
Road freight brakemen and flagmen (local and way)	15,056	16,265
Yard conductors and yard firemen	13,695	21,194
Yard brakemen and yard helpers	36,416	54,485
Road passenger engineers and motormen	8,678	7,959
Road freight engineers and motormen (through)	12,630	14,204
Road freight engineers and motormen (local and way)	6,556	7,453
Yard engineers and motormen	13,248	18,648
Road passenger firemen and helpers	7,933	7,353
Road freight firemen and helpers (through)	14,780	15,550
Road freight firemen and helpers (local and way)	7,119	7,717
Yard firemen and helpers	14,483	19,610

Source: I.C.C. Statement No. M-300, 1939 and December, 1952.

METHODS OF WAGE PAYMENT

The methods of wage payment can again be considered from the point of view of nonoperating and operating workers. With respect to the former group, the provisions of the agreements are similar in many respects to those covering other industrial workers. The latter group, however, over the years, has developed a set of complicated rules governing the method by which its members are paid.

With few exceptions, all nonoperating workers are paid on an hourly, weekly, or monthly basis. Eight hours represent a basic work day, and since September 1, 1949, the nonoperating workers have been on a five-day week. Overtime beyond the eight hours and work on the two consecutive days off after five days of work is paid for at time-and-one-half rates. No punitive pay rates, that is, double time for work on Saturdays, Sundays, and holidays, are paid.[18]

The wage-and-hour rules applicable to the operating group can be broken down into the following categories:

1. Road employees.—This group of workers, which includes engineers, firemen, enginemen, conductors, and trainmen, is paid on the so-called "dual basis," that is, they are paid on a mileage basis but "if it takes longer than a certain time to run the miles paid for, then they receive overtime in addition to payment for the mileage made." [19]

However, what constitutes a day's work differs for various groups. For all employees in the road freight service the basic day consists of "eight hours or less—100 miles or less." Thus, for all excess mileage beyond 100, the employee is paid $\frac{1}{100}$ of the basic daily rate for each mile. However, if the run takes longer than eight hours, time and a half for overtime is paid "only when the miles run divided by the time of duty produce a ratio less than the speed basis," that is, $12\frac{1}{2}$ miles per hour. For example, if a 125-mile run takes ten hours, payment is made on a straight mileage basis (since the average speed of $12\frac{1}{2}$ miles per hour was maintained); but if it takes eleven hours to complete a 125-mile run, the employee is paid for 125 miles on a "straight-time" basis and time and a half for one hour of overtime.[20]

Similar methods of wage payment are used with respect to the other types of workers in the "road group" except that in the passenger service—distinguished from the freight service described above—the basic day for engineers and firemen is 100 miles or five hours, and for conductors and trainmen, 150 miles or seven and a half hours. The method for computing overtime is essentially the same as that for road freight workers. The engineer's and firemen's rates vary not only in accordance with the type and weight of the locomotive but

EMPLOYMENT 23

also in accordance with the class of service rendered, e.g., road freight or local freight.[21]

One variation in overtime payment is the so-called "8 within 9" rule, applicable to short turn-around passenger runs. Under this rule "over-time is independent of speed or miles run." Overtime begins automatically at the end of the ninth hour after the employee goes on duty. Meanwhile, the employee draws straight-time pay for eight hours, and overtime pay for any time on duty or held for duty, exceeding eight hours, within the nine-hour period. After the ninth hour, his overtime runs continuously until final release, though he may not operate a train until the tenth or eleventh hour after first going on duty.[22] In all cases, an employee receives at least a basic day's pay regardless of the number of hours worked or the miles covered.[23]

In many agreements the number of miles run by, say, an engineer or a fireman, is limited. This, of course, limits his earnings. Such mileage limitations in effect have the result of spreading work among certain types of workers, particularly those who are employed in the operation of fast moving trains. Although the mileage limitations vary somewhat on different railroads, generally they are 4,800 miles per month for regular engineers and firemen in freight service. Where limitations apply to trainmen, the maximum runs from about 5,500 to 6,600 miles per month for passenger trainmen and 3,500 to 4,500 miles per month for freight trainmen.[24]

In addition to the wage payment, railroad employees, particularly those in the operating group, receive certain "arbitraries" or "constructive allowances." For example, the dual method of payment for so-called "road" men provides for extra payments for straight-time excess mileage within the hour limits and such "extras" are recorded by the Interstate Commerce Commission as payments for hours not worked. Thus, if a conductor in the through freight service runs 125 miles in eight hours, the records of the I.C.C. will show a payment for ten hours of work, and will record eight hours of actual work.[25] A study made in 1934 reveals that about one fourth of the discrepancy between "hours worked" and "hours paid for" is explained by the daily or monthly guarantees (regardless of hours or days worked) and the remaining three fourths by the method of recording straight-time excess mileage.[26]

One impartial student has observed that in essence the dual system of wage payments is a pure rate system. "If criticism is to be levied, it should obviously be directed against the prevailing unit wage rates and the size of the standard unit of output. These are the results of negotiation between the carriers and the employees" and not the result of the *method* of payment.[27]

Although the railroads are critical of this method of wage payment and make frequent references to the fact that they pay wages for hours not worked, it is interesting to note that the dual system of wage payment was sought by the railroads when a hundred miles was regarded as "a fair day's work." [28] Apparently it was also approved by the labor organizations in order to prevent abuses on the part of the train dispatchers who had the workers at their mercy with respect to hours. However, with the advent of faster trains the hundred-mile limit for the engineers and firemen has become outmoded and obsolete. Yet despite the criticism by the railroads, they have not sought to change these rates in the recent wage and rules movements. Nor have they sought the elimination of the dual system of wage payment.[29]

2. The Yardmen.—This group includes those employees who work within the railroad yards—engineers, firemen, conductors, brakemen, and switchmen. These workers, of course, cannot be paid on a mileage basis and therefore are paid on an hourly basis, with the usual daily guarantees. Overtime is paid at a rate of time and a half, with the length of the work week varying on different railroads. No premium rates exist

for work on Saturday, Sundays, and holidays. The wages of engineers and firemen in the yard, though on an hourly basis, also vary in accordance with the type and weight of the locomotive.

From the description given above of the methods of wage payment and hours of work, one can observe certain problems which impinge on the industrial relations of the railroad industry.

In the first place, the dual method of payment for many road employees has rewarded this group of workers for increased productivity resulting from technological changes in the form of greater speed of the locomotives. Such reward, though not necessarily reflected in higher pay, is at least found in a shorter work week. In addition, with the trend toward heavier locomotives over the years,[30] the engineers and firemen have been able to obtain higher wages. Such rewards for increased productivity have not been given to yard workers, though some, such as yard engineers and firemen, are paid according to the weight of the locomotive. Thus, given the propensity of workers to indulge in the comparison of wages, it is natural that certain disgruntlements may arise. In fact, one railroad union official of an organization covering certain yard workers once stated to the writer that he thought that over the years the group of workers whom he represented may have been "hurt" (i.e., they did not get the wages they should have) by participating jointly with other unions in concerted movements. One reason was that the higher pay of roadmen, resulting from these technological changes, when described by railroad management before an emergency board, influenced the recommendations of the board.

A second serious problem has arisen over the question of hours. A large number of the roadmen are, in effect, working less than forty hours a week because of the nature of their work. In 1949, the nonoperating workers were granted a forty-hour work week *with the maintenance of take-home pay,* in addition to a wage increase.[31] A forty-hour work week for yard workers was recommended by an emergency board, but *without* the maintenance of take-home pay. A wage increase of 18 cents an hour was recommended—13 cents less than the hourly sum necessary to maintain the take-home pay on the basis of a forty-hour work week.[32] The unions rejected that board's recommendations and the government seized the railroads after a strike occurred. Regardless of the merits of the issue, it is apparent that the yard workers think that they are being discriminated against in comparison with other railroad workers, and with virtually all other industrial workers as well.[33]

A third problem arising from the variety of methods of wage payment has been the method of application of wage increases. For example, if a wage increase of, say, $1.60 per day is finally agreed upon for the operating workers, the yardmen on an eight-hour day obtain an increase of 20 cents an hour. However, since the engineers' and firemen's basic work day is five hours (for through passenger trains) they, in effect, obtain an increase of 32 cents an hour. As a result, some railroad workers note that they must work more hours than others to obtain the same wage increase.

Working Rules

The working rules in the railroad industry have developed over the years for reasons similar to those which brought about working rules in other industries. These rules, which will be described below, reflect, according to Slichter, "the desire of the workers for protection against the arbitrary and uncontrolled discretion of management." In addition, the rules provide some protection for the union organization, "allocate limited opportunities to work," and protect the workers "against the cost and impact of technological change." Thus, the elaborate system of working rules in the railroad industry has developed out of the needs and demands of the workers, who have been confronted with technological changes and declining employment opportunities. Management also has need for a set of working rules for operating purposes. It becomes concerned, however, when these rules are obsolete, thereby retarding output and efficiency.[34]

The working rules of the nonoperating workers in the railroad industry are similar in many respects to those covering other industrial workers. However, the rules applicable to the operating workers are more elaborate and complex, and in view of the fact that the "rules problem" in the industry involves the operating workers more than others, an examination of the rules affecting the latter group is in order. It should be noted that a completely detailed description of all of the rules is virtually impossible because of their technicalities and complexities, but the basic nature of the more important rules —their importance measured by the extent of controversy they have precipitated—will be presented.

THE ORIGIN OF THE WORKING RULES

It is obvious that the operations of the railroad system require a set of rules by which to guide the activities of the workers. The original working rules were nothing more than oral instructions issued by the supervisory employees of the carriers.[35] With the growth and development of the railroad system these oral instructions were superseded by written statements posted on bulletin boards. Subsequently, management printed and issued rule books in order to standardize these instructions throughout the railroad systems. Finally, with the advent and growth of railroad labor organizations, their representatives demanded that they be allowed to participate in the writing of the rules. These rules were eventually embodied in the collective bargaining agreements. Today negotiations over the working rules have become an important aspect of collective bargaining in the railroad industry.

There have been, to all intents and purposes, five national rules movements in which the railroad workers sought the extension and broadening of the working rules.[36] The first movement began in 1907 and continued until 1916. During this period the labor organizations sought revisions and additions to the working rules. Most of the disputes were settled by voluntary arbitration under the provisions of the Erdman Act and the Newlands Act.[37] A total of ten arbitration proceedings were held to resolve the issues.[38]

The second rules movement started after the passage of the Adamson Act in 1916 and ended when the federal government took over the control of the railroads in 1917.[39] The Adamson Act, as will be noted in the following chapter, provided that "eight hours shall . . . be deemed a day's work and the measure or standard of a day's work for the purpose of reckoning the compensation for services of all [railroad] employees." [40] The railroads refused to put the eight-hour work day into effect, asserting that the law was unconstitutional. Although the Supreme Court eventually ruled in 1917 that the law was constitutional, the threat of a strike while the issue was still before the courts resulted in the settlement of the question on March 19, 1917, by "The Committee of the Council of National Defence." [41] This Committee established a basic eight-hour work day, as provided under the Adamson Act, spelled out the application of the basic eight-hour-work-day principle to the workers in the road service, and established a bipartisan Commission of Eight to resolve all disputes arising out of the application of the award. The Commission arranged meetings between the carriers and the labor organizations in order to determine the application of the Council's award to the individual contracts. On the basis of these discussions, the Commission of Eight issued decisions and interpretations which were applicable to yardmen and roadmen and which were concerned with such questions as hours of duty, starting time, "held away from terminal rules," and monthly guarantees.[42]

The third rules movement took place during the period of federal control of the railroads, from 1918 to 1920. During this three-year period the Director General issued many orders in an attempt to standardize and codify the then existing working rules. These changes were incorporated in national agreements signed by the Director General and applicable to all railroads under government operation. A Board of Railroad Wages and Working Conditions was also established for the purpose of adjusting disputes arising out of the interpretation and application of the working rules.[43] It was during this period that the railroad labor organizations made considerable progress in securing new rules and broad interpretations of existing rules for their own protection and benefit. Although a great many of these "national" contracts were not renewed when the railroads were returned to private control, the precedents established on many railroads were carried over and still exist in a large number of agreements in force today.

The fourth rules movement was initiated by the railroad labor organizations after the enactment of the Transportation Act of 1920.[44] As noted in the following chapter, the Act provided for the establishment of a Railroad Labor Board, the main function of which was to handle all types of disputes which were not resolved by the parties by direct negotiation. Thus the Board was concerned not only with disputes over wages and working conditions but was also responsible for adjusting grievances which might arise out of the interpretation and application of the working rules as embodied in the collective bargaining agreements. For reasons that are discussed in the following chapter, the railroad workers were dissatisfied with the administration of the law. The operating workers were unsuccessful in their attempts to revise and extend the working rules. However, the nonoperating workers secured several favorable decisions concerning the subcontracting of work to firms outside of the railroad industry.

The fifth rules movement started after the passage of the amendments to the Railway Labor Act in 1934. The railroads claim that "this fifth rules movement differed from all other rules movements in that it did not involve rewriting any rule or amending the language contained in any schedule; but by a process of interpreting existing rules, the Adjustment Board [established by the 1934 amendments] since 1934, has completely changed the entire meaning and effect of many rules and practices of long standing, and has immeasurably increased the control of the Organizations over railway operations and the featherbedding incident to the application of the Operating Employees Rules." A similar extension of the scope of the rules has been made for clerical workers and telegraphers. It is suggested by the railroads that the reason for this development is not the fault of the Adjustment Board but rather a reflection of the fact that the original contracts, or schedules, were written by laymen but the interpretations of the language have been made by referees who are usually lawyers by training and who have at times twisted the meaning of the language.[45]

The Adjustment Board is given an opportunity to interpret the working rules when claims are brought before it by representatives of the employees. These claims are either "denied" or "allowed" by the Board, whose award, based on its opinion or interpretation of the working rule, may provide (and has provided) a basis for a flood of new claims. The role of the Adjustment Board in the handling of grievances brought before it, as well as the attempt of the railroads to reduce their costs, have been important factors in the movement of the carriers to relax or eliminate the working rules.[46]

Thus, there has been a gradual evolution in the working rules since the turn of the century. These rules have been em-

EMPLOYMENT 31

bodied in the collective bargaining agreements as a result of direct negotiations between the parties, the intervention of the government, and "interpretations" by the National Railroad Adjustment Board, whose voice has frequently been the voice of the referee. The change in the breadth and scope of the rules is revealed by the fact that at the beginning of the century a typical set of working rules covered about six printed pages. Today, one collective bargaining agreement between a labor organization and an eastern railroad consists of 248 printed pages.[47]

What is the nature of these working rules? What has been the role of the Adjustment Board in their development? How have the carriers sought the relaxation or elimination of these rules? How successful have they been? What effect has the working rules problem had upon collective bargaining? These questions will be discussed below.

THE NATURE OF THE WORKING RULES [48]

The working rules, which are generally applicable to the carriers and their employees and which have been subject to the greatest controversy in recent years, are concerned with operations, the assignment of work, the use of equipment, the manning of equipment, and the payment of certain "arbitraries and special allowances." Each of these categories will be discussed in turn.

Operations. Many carriers, under the rules and on the basis of interpretations of the National Railroad Adjustment Board, do not have the right to establish or eliminate yard service or yard assignments as they see fit. Thus, once any yard service is provided or any yard assignment is made, the railroads may not eliminate any such service or assignments. In one award the National Railroad Adjustment Board ruled that "in scores of cases, including decisions by six Referees, this Division has held that yard work as to which seniority is held by yardmen cannot be taken away from them and turned over to roadmen to perform. Whether it be so expressly stipulated in the schedule or not, is not controlling . . . since the work is the very subject matter of the contract with the yardmen, and to hold it to be the prerogative of one party to the contract to destroy the subject matter of it would be to hold that no contract exists." [49] Under this ruling the carriers must maintain a full crew and pay them for eight hours of work under the daily guarantee in instances where, say, one hour of switching service is required each day. They cannot employ roadmen for this service. In a few instances, the operating unions and the carriers have negotiated agreements which provide for the establishment or cutting off of yard crews based on the amount of switching service necessary.

The carriers did not have, until recently, any flexibility in the establishment of the yard limits which fix the boundaries between yard and road work. Thus, if switching service were required beyond the yard limits, road crews had to be employed for that service, except in emergencies. The Adjustment Board had ruled that established boundaries could be changed only as a result of "negotiation and agreement between the parties." [50] Failure to comply with this rule, and subject to the interpretations of the National Railroad Adjustment Board as to whether or not an "emergency" existed, the carriers have found themselves liable for triple payments, although only one service is performed (the road crew receives two days' pay and the yard crew, which would have performed the service, receives one day's pay). The 1950, 1951, and 1952 settlements permitted some changes in switching and yard limits under certain circumstances.

Railroad management is required, in accordance with most agreements, to start the work shifts of the yardmen within certain specified hours and assignments cannot be changed without forty-eight hours' notice. Here, too, the carriers lose a certain amount of flexibility of operation.

The right of many carriers to establish interdivisional runs

EMPLOYMENT 33

is limited by the working rules and the interpretations of the Adjustment Board. In the early years of the railroads a typical day's run was about a hundred miles and therefore divisional points were established where crews changed and inspections and servicing took place. With the introduction of diesel locomotives and the increasing speed of the trains, the railroads now find it desirable to establish interdivisional runs, that is, runs spanning more than one division. Such interdivisional runs would result in savings to the carriers. The railroads have argued that they have the right to establish interdivisional runs as long as there is "an equalization of mileage to conform with seniority rights," but the Adjustment Board has ruled that, where existing rules cover the subject, interdivisional runs cannot be established "except by agreement, because to do so would be destructive of the seniority provisions of the agreement."[51] On some railroads, however, the agreements permit the carriers to establish interdivisional runs without the necessity of securing the approval of the labor organizations.

Assignment of Work. The carriers, under the rules, may not assign roadmen to perform any yard work, and conversely, yardmen may not be assigned to do road work. If this is done the carriers become subject to penalty payments. This principle has been upheld by the rulings of the Adjustment Board.[52] However, road freight crews may perform switching service at a limited number of intermediate points where no yard crews are assigned and are paid the higher local freight rates instead of through freight rates. Similarly, the handling of engines within the yard must be assigned to yardmen and not to roadmen. In addition, the railroads are prevented in many instances from using yardmen or trainmen to couple and uncouple air hose and to make air tests but must use carmen whenever the latter are available. The railroads find themselves subject to the interpretations of the Adjustment Board as to what is meant by "the availability of carmen" and may at times find themselves in a position where "extra" payments for the service must be made.[53] Finally, supervisory employees are prevented from performing incidental engine, train, or yard service.[54]

The railroads may not employ yard workers on a second shift within a twenty-four-hour period unless they pay time and a half for the second shift. They are also prevented from using a member of a crew in other work. If they do, according to the interpretations of the Adjustment Board, the carriers might have to pay the employee separated from his crew an extra day's pay.

Use of Equipment. Although there is no typical pattern, certain railroads are subject to state laws and working rules which "limit the length of a train, specify the number of employees, limit the number of locomotives or cars or the amount of tonnage that may be handled in one train, or which provide extra compensation for members of the crew by reason of the number of locomotives or cars or amount of tonnage handled in such trains." [55]

In some instances, the carriers must pay the higher rate of pay when the employees are engaged in, say, two classes of freight service. In one case, when some freight cars were attached to a passenger train, the employee was paid the higher rate.[56]

Manning of Equipment. On some railroads the composition or "consist" of crews in the yard and road service is spelled out. Thus, the carriers are prevented from varying the "consist" in accordance with their requirements. Similarly, the carriers are prevented, on the basis of the rulings of the Adjustment Board, from using maintenance of way crews in the movement of certain types of equipment (such as self-propelled equipment) and are required to use both maintenance of way crews and train-service employees when the equipment is in use. The Adjustment Board has made frequent awards "in cases both where there was, and where there

EMPLOYMENT 35

was not, a special agreement covering" the use of such equipment.[57]

Arbitraries and Special Allowances. These types of payments involve what the railroads frequently refer to as "wages paid for work not done." They include the following: payments for delay before the departure of the train, delay at the final terminal, side trips off the main line, and deadheading, that is, payment to an employee who is simply being transported back to the point from which he started his run.

A common rule is the so-called "conversion" or "more than one class of service" rule which requires the railroads to pay the highest rate when two types of service are performed. The railroads suggest that in rare cases "if a company letter were carried in the coat pocket of the attendant in charge of the baggage car, all employees assigned to the train would receive the local freight rate rather than the rate applicable to the class of service to which they were assigned." [58] In some instances when two types of service, unrelated to each other, are performed, the railroads are required to make two payments and sometimes three. The latter situation develops when the worker involved receives two days' pay, one day at each of the applicable rates, and the worker who should have performed the service receives a day's pay.[59]

The purpose of these rules must be distinguished from their effect. As to purpose, the employees, on one hand, assert that the working rules are designed to prevent abuses on the part of management in the allocation and assignment of work and to provide an incentive to the railroads (via penalty payments) for the improvement of the operations of the railroads. The carriers, on the other hand, urge that the working rules, as revised and extended through the years, represent nothing more than an attempt on the part of the employees to obtain higher wages and to maintain the level of their employment in the face of technological changes. There are elements of truth in both viewpoints.

The effect of the rules, from the labor organizations' point of view, is that the workers receive extra compensation and are given a greater degree of security. From the carriers' point of view, the rules prevent them from obtaining the cost reductions, which flow from mechanization, and limit the flexibility of railroad operations.

During the past fifteen years the railroads have initiated movements to eliminate or relax the existing rules. To counteract this and to offset the decline in employment in the industry, the labor organizations have sought to extend the working rules.

RECENT RULES MOVEMENTS

To change the working rules the carriers have, in accordance with the procedures under the Railway Labor Act, as amended, attempted at first to negotiate "on the properties." The adamant position of the labor organizations that such rules changes are not feasible and that they would destroy rights and privileges obtained after many years of bargaining has prevented the settlement of the issue by direct negotiation between the parties. Mediation, too, has been unsuccessful, so that the issues eventually have been presented to emergency boards established by the President (in accordance with the provisions of the Railway Labor Act). As will be noted below, the handling of the working rules' issue by emergency boards has not been successful: first, the boards themselves have frequently found that the issues are too complex and intricate to be decided by persons not personally familiar with the history and origin of the working rules; second, the labor organizations have refused to present evidence on the demands of the carriers for changes in the working rules; third, the unions have rejected the boards' recommendations in many instances and the final settlement has usually resulted in a wage increase and a moratorium on changes in the working rules. Thus, collective bargaining be-

EMPLOYMENT 37

tween the parties on the working rules is virtually nonexistent nor is the machinery under the Railway Labor Act, as amended, adequate to handle this problem. The result has been a virtual stalemate.

In 1937 the carriers started a movement to revise the working rules. The labor organizations countered with a demand for higher wages and refused to discuss the rules problem. The final agreement involved solely the question of wages.[60] In 1938, the railroads sought a wage reduction and the emergency board established by the President rejected the railroads' request. But in the course of its report, the board suggested that some of the working rules be relaxed or eliminated so that the carriers could reduce their costs.[61]

The railroads were apparently encouraged by this suggestion and after extensive investigation served notice on the labor organizations in May and June 1941, requesting the elimination of what they referred to as "objectionable" rules. During the proceedings, the labor organizations served notice of their desire for an extension of working rules. In the eyes of the carriers this was simply a maneuver to offset the carriers' request.[62] The dispute was finally settled by mediation by an emergency board. Under the settlement the workers received a wage increase and both sides agreed to a moratorium on rule changes during the emergency period.[63]

In its original report, which was rejected by the labor organizations, the 1941 board noted that the carriers had urged that the board not "consider the merits of the specific rules proposed" but rather that the board find that negotiations had not been carried on in good faith.[64] The carriers urged that the board recommend that, if further negotiation were unsuccessful, mediation and eventually arbitration be employed when necessary. The unions opposed this suggestion of the carriers. The board called for a "re-examination" of the rules so as to permit the railroads to adapt themselves to "new" conditions and suggested that the procedures under the Railway Labor Act be followed.

In 1943 the railroad labor organizations sought a wage increase. The carriers did not counter with a demand for the relaxation or elimination of certain working rules because of the existing rules moratorium. During the course of the proceedings, however, the labor organizations sought certain rules changes in order to circumvent the stabilization program which, under the Little Steel formula, limited the wage increase which could be granted to the railroad workers. The eventual settlement of the case, after the intervention of the President, provided for additional money in lieu of time and a half for overtime after forty hours and expenses away from home (both of which were requested by the unions) and ignored changes in the rules.[65]

In 1945–1946 the railroads again sought changes in the existing rules. The labor organizations countered with a demand for a wage increase and a request for an extension of the scope of the rules. The entire case went before an emergency board which pointed out in its report that the forty-four proposals of the labor organizations and the twenty-nine proposals of the carriers for rules changes were of such complexity that it did not feel competent to make recommendations on all of the proposals.[66] The board made recommendations favorable to both sides. It noted that both sides failed to negotiate the proposals in good faith. The report of the board, which also recommended a wage increase, was rejected by the employees and the final settlement included a wage increase larger than that recommended by the board and a one year moratorium on rules changes.[67]

In 1947 the carriers instituted negotiations for the elimination of certain rules. The unions, in turn, requested both a wage increase and the broadening of the scope of the rules. The emergency board, established by the President to consider the issues, carefully examined the requests for rules changes and made recommendations—some of which were favorable to management, others favorable to labor—at the same time urging the withdrawal of the requests for some rules changes.[68] In its report the board noted that the representatives of the labor organizations refused to submit any evidence on the carriers' requests. The board was particularly concerned with the fact that the parties failed to negotiate many of the rules changes "on the properties." It pointed out:

> . . . to use the Emergency Board procedure in this fashion seems to defeat its purpose. . . . The time which was spent in trying to follow through all the minutiae . . . unsifted by the parties themselves during two years of bargaining, was time that could otherwise have been devoted to resolving the issues of basic principle. . . . It is a mistake to call upon a Board such as this, as part of an . . . emergency procedure, to spend its time trying to unravel a tangle of wrapping string. That these parties were not able to accomplish by negotiation, even this little kitchen job, is cause for real concern. In our judgment this kind of failure has, so far as collective bargaining is concerned, malignant potentialities. . . .
> We repeat that the weakening of collective bargaining . . . was manifest as well in too many of the other issues in this case. We urge upon the parties that they start revitalizing the cooperative element in their relationship by working out satisfactory settlements of those issues which cannot possibly be disposed of properly here.[69]

The recommendations of the board were rejected by the unions, and the case was eventually settled after the intervention of the President.

The same sequence of events took place in 1949–1950, and again the emergency board rejected virtually all of the requests of the railroads for changes in the working rules but urged that the parties negotiate the issues and, if settlement did not result, submit the rules changes to arbitration.[70] The board, however, supported the demand of the labor organizations for a forty-hour work week, but did not provide for the maintenance of take-home pay. The labor organizations refused to accept the recommendations and after a series of strikes and the seizure of the railroads by the federal government, the unions settled with the carriers. Under the settlements the labor organizations yielded on several of the demands of the carriers for changes in the rules (with respect to switching and yard limits) and agreed to submit to arbitration the so-called "more than one class of service rule." The arbitration award, as mentioned previously, modified the rule.

As has been indicated above, the emergency boards have in general been extremely reluctant to make recommendations with respect to changes in the working rules and have frequently urged the parties to negotiate on the issues. However, in discussing the carriers' proposals for changes in the working rules the emergency boards have, in some instances, indicated that there is considerable merit in their position and have recently, in a few cases, made specific recommendations.

In 1948 an emergency board, for example, refused to make any recommendations with respect to the establishment of interdivisional runs but pointed out that both parties were adhering to extreme positions and that it was in the public interest that the issue be settled by the parties themselves.[71] On the question of establishing time limits in which claims could be filed the board made specific recommendations.[72] The board stated that such questions as the employment of trainmen for coupling and uncoupling hose, the right of management to adjust the switching and yard limits, the right of management to employ supervisory personnel for incidental tasks in the yards, and the relaxation of the conversion rule, should be handled by bargaining between the parties.[73]

In 1950, the emergency board considered the rules changes requested by the carriers and was impressed by the need for

EMPLOYMENT 41

eliminating the restrictions against interdivisional runs, easing the rule on coupling and uncoupling air hose, and giving management the right to revise switching limits in accordance with its needs.[74] However, the board simply urged that the parties negotiate these changes. If the parties were unable to agree on the rules changes the board suggested that they agree to arbitrate the dispute.[75] The unions rejected the board's report, but subsequently the Switchmen's Union of North America settled its case with the railroads and agreed to allow management the right to expand switching limits and further agreed to permit switchmen to couple or uncouple air hose for a specific rate of compensation. The brotherhoods of firemen, engineers, and trainmen, in their settlements, accepted the revised switching limit rule and agreed to arbitrate the "coupling and uncoupling of air hose" and the conversion issues. The arbitration awards were favorable to the carriers, and were the first successful attempt to relax the working rules.[76]

THE EFFECT OF THE WORKING RULES PROBLEM ON COLLECTIVE BARGAINING

In view of their financial problem the railroads naturally are seeking reductions in their costs of operation. The increasing mechanization of the railroads threatens the employment opportunities of the railroad workers. The railroads, in an attempt to improve their financial position and to obtain the greatest benefits from their mechanization program, have sought the elimination or relaxation of many of the working rules. The unions, sensing a threat not only to their employment but also to their labor organizations as institutions, seek the tightening or extension of the rules. What has been the effect of this conflict on the collective bargaining relationships in the railroad industry?

It has been pointed out above that the unions simply refuse to bargain on rules changes, although there has been a slight change in this attitude recently, at least with respect to a few of the rules. The carriers, therefore, have no alternative but to utilize the procedures of the Railway Labor Act, as amended, and to invoke mediation, which is conducted by the National Mediation Board. In view of the attitudes of the parties, mediation has not been successful and therefore the President has established emergency boards to consider the rules changes. These boards, as has been indicated, are reluctant to handle this type of question because of the complexities and intricacies of the rules. They have generally urged that rules changes be negotiated or, if collective bargaining fails, be subject to arbitration. The unions, fearful of so-called "outsiders," have generally refused to submit these questions to arbitration. The result is an impasse. One may conclude generally that there has been no genuine collective bargaining on working rules in the railroad industry for fifteen or twenty years.

As is suggested in Chapter XI, the National Railroad Adjustment Board has not adequately handled the grievance disputes which arise out of the interpretation and application of the working rules as they are embodied in the collective bargaining agreements. The labor organizations have been successful in obtaining interpretations of the working rules which have benefitted the employees and which, at times, have given rise to new claims. (Each railroad has been reluctant to settle claims on the property, apparently fearful that any interpretation on its part might be used by the unions for application on other railroads.) The unions, therefore, have been forced to submit grievances to the Adjustment Board for decision. The result has been a large accumulation of undecided grievance disputes. The unions, facing delay in the disposition of the grievance disputes, have sought other means for their settlement (via strike action), the emergency board procedures of the Railway Labor Act, or even the courts. From 1945 to 1950 the emergency board route was generally followed. The original framers of the law did not contemplate the use of emergency boards for the settlement of grievance disputes. Furthermore, such boards are not the proper forum before which such disputes should be presented for settlement. Rather, grievance disputes should be resolved by negotiation between the parties or by decision of the Adjustment Board, as provided by law. This practice, of bringing grievance disputes before emergency boards, had practically ceased during 1951 and the first half of 1952 primarily because the carriers have been under Army control.[77] With the return of the railroads to private owners in May 1952, strikes and threatened strikes over grievances have broken out anew.

Thus, we find a breakdown in collective bargaining between the parties with respect to working rules as well as with respect to grievance disputes arising out of those rules. And this breakdown in collective bargaining is a factor in the explanation of the unstable labor relations in the railroad industry, particularly with respect to the operating workers.

Conclusion

It has been noted in this chapter that prior to the outbreak of World War II employment in the railroad industry was constantly declining. The revival in employment during World War II and for a brief period after the outbreak of the Korean War was short-lived. In fact, the revival in employment of the operating workers was relatively small and it is in this area where the conflict between the carriers and their employees is sharpest. When this long-run decline in employment is considered along with the difficult financial condition and increasing mechanization of the railroads, the concern of the workers over the working rules and the desire on the part of the carriers for the revision or elimination of these rules become understandable. The elaborate methods of wage payment and the complex working rules mean more money and greater security to the workers; to the railroads they mean higher costs.

The importance of these wage and working rules to both parties is clear. The unions refuse to negotiate any changes, except to make the rules more restrictive. The railroads find that the National Railroad Adjustment Board has in many instances extended the scope of the rules and that the emergency boards, which have from time to time considered the issues, generally do not feel competent to handle questions of such great complexity and wide implication. When emergency boards have made recommendations on rules changes, the labor organizations have usually rejected such recommendations. The net effect has been the virtual collapse of collective bargaining between the operating unions and the carriers on the issue of working rules.

CHAPTER IV

THE LABOR ORGANIZATIONS

OF THE more than 1,200,000 workers employed in the railroad industry in 1952, about 75 to 80 percent are members of the various labor organizations.[1] Over fifty labor organizations are listed by the National Mediation Board as having collective labor agreements with 136 selected railroads.[2] These labor organizations include, however, a large number which represent very small groups of workers. Essentially, there are twenty-two standard railroad labor organizations, of which five, sometimes referred to as the "Big Five," represent those workers—conductors, trainmen, engineers, firemen, hostlers, and switchmen—who "are engaged in the actual physical movement of trains and cars." [3] Approximately 22 percent of the railroad workers are in this category, commonly referred to as the "operating" group.[4] The other seventeen labor organizations, sometimes referred to as the "Seventeen Cooperating Railway Labor Organizations," represent those workers "engaged in clerical and office duties, construction and maintenance of the equipment or rolling stock, operation and maintenance of signal and telegraphic systems, the general servicing of the railroad plant, and operation of stations and yards." [5] This group is usually referred to as the "nonoperating" workers.

It is the purpose of this chapter, first, to describe the labor organizations included in each of these two groups; second, to indicate the militancy of, and the interunion conflicts among, the labor organizations, particularly the unions involving the "operating" workers; and third, to suggest that this militancy and these conflicts are significant factors in the unstable labor relations in the railroad industry.

The Operating Unions

The five operating labor organizations and their estimated membership (in 1944) include: [6]

Brotherhood of Railroad Trainmen	196,000
Brotherhood of Locomotive Firemen and Enginemen	120,200
Brotherhood of Locomotive Engineers	75,800
Order of Railway Conductors of America	42,000
Switchmen's Union of North America	9,300

Of these five unions, only one—the Switchmen's Union of North America—is affiliated with the American Federation of Labor; the other four have been independent since their inception. Despite efforts of the AF of L to woo the four unions into its organization, they have remained aloof because of a feeling of superior status: they consider themselves not only the aristocrats of railway labor,[7] but also the aristocrats of all labor, because of their relatively high earning power.[8] It is this historical background of "superior status" which, when related to "the deterioration of their relative earning status" (discussed in Chapter VIII), may explain the militant attitude of the railroad labor leaders today.[9]

Another factor to be considered in analyzing the reasons for the militancy of the operating unions is the historical background of wage cuts in depressions, court injunctions, the use of the militia in strikes, the use of violence, and the hostility of management toward the workers.[10] Against this background the present militancy of these unions can be at least understood, even if not condoned.

Although there is a prevailing popular impression that the operating unions tend to act in concert—at least with respect to national movements on wages and working conditions—there are, on the contrary, "over-lapping interests, jealousies, and . . . frequent conflicts" and "occasionally members of one organization [have] acted as strikebreakers" in disputes involving a sister organization.[11] For example, the Brotherhood of Railroad Trainmen has contracts covering road conductors, yard workers, road brakemen, flagmen and baggagemen and dining car stewards. As a result, this organization comes into frequent conflict with such organizations as the Order of Railway Conductors, and the Switchmen's Union of North America. Similarly, there is some overlapping between the Brotherhood of Locomotive Engineers and the Brotherhood of Locomotive Firemen and Enginemen.[12] All attempts at industrial unionism, the system plan of federation, and "the association plan, with the national unions as participating units" have failed.[13]

The operating unions and the nonoperating unions have carried on negotiations with the railroads on a nationwide basis several times in the past two decades, but such bargaining has been concerned, except in one case, with questions of maintenance of employment, retirement plans, and general legislation. In 1932, the Railway Labor Executives' Association, which comprises twenty railroad labor organizations (the nonoperating labor organizations and the switchmen's union are at present affiliated with this body) and which is concerned chiefly with legislative matters, participated in negotiating the wage reduction of 1932, covering all workers, both operating and nonoperating. Furthermore, the "Washington Job Protection Agreement," which provides protection for employees "who are retained after a consolidation or merger of railroads," was negotiated by the railroad labor organizations as a group with the carriers. This job protection, which involves certain allowances being paid to separated workers, was, in the main, included in the Transportation Act of 1940.[14] Finally, in 1937, the organizations as a group worked out, with the agreement of the carriers, plans for retirement benefits and unemployment compensation, and these plans were enacted into law.[15]

With respect to bargaining on wages and working conditions, at least in recent years, railroad labor has split itself into operating and nonoperating groups. This grouping may reflect the "superior status" attitude on the part of the operating workers. It may also reflect the fact that the operating workers have a superior strategic bargaining power because the special skills of the operating workers are not required in any other labor market, with the result that there is no other source of labor for strike-breaking activities in the event of a strike. The skills of most of the nonoperating workers are generally such as may exist among workers doing similar types of work in other industries. This conclusion may be confirmed, in part, by the fact that in recent years the serious threats to the operations of the railroads have come from the operating groups and not from the so-called "nonops."

Even the five operating unions have not been a cohesive group. Rather, the number and the particular organizations participating in concerted wage and rules movements have been rather fluid. The concerted wage movement began at the turn of the century and has, with few exceptions, continued to date. The considerations involved in the "make-up" of these movements have probably been political in nature —political from the point of view of the leadership of the labor organizations. Since the 1934 amendments to the Railway Labor Act, the following concerted wage movements took place with the alignments described below:

1. In March, 1937, the five operating unions presented demands for a 20 percent wage increase. This case was eventually settled as a result of mediation.[16]

2. In 1938, four operating unions (exclusive of the Brotherhood of Railroad Trainmen) and fourteen nonoperating unions participated in a wage movement which eventually resulted in a hearing before an emergency board and succeeded in preventing the imposition of a wage cut.[17]

3. In 1941, the operating unions, consisting of the five operating organizations, and the fourteen nonoperating, filed separate demands for wage increases. When the parties failed to settle the case, the services of an emergency board were invoked by the President to consider the issues of both groups.[18]

4. In 1943, the five operating unions again requested a wage increase from the carriers. Although the case was eventually settled after a report was issued by an emergency board,[19] threatened strikes, and government seizure, serious splits and difficulties developed in the conduct of the negotiations. The history of the conflict has been presented by one side, and in the report issued by the Brotherhood of Locomotive Firemen and Enginemen, Order of Railway Conductors, and the Switchmen's Union, the words "betrayal," "sell-out," and "bad faith" appear repeatedly when references are made to the Brotherhood of Railroad Trainmen and the Brotherhood of Locomotive Engineers. There were conflicts over the conduct of the hearings as well as the handling of negotiations in the White House in an attempt to settle the dispute.[20]

5. In 1945, the five operating unions submitted demands upon the carriers for wage increases, but during the process of mediation three unions—the conductors, the enginemen and the switchmen—agreed to arbitrate the dispute while the wage and rule demands of the engineers and trainmen were presented to an emergency board.[21]

6. In 1949, the railroad conductors and the trainmen (who had not joined in the previous two movements) jointly presented demands for changes in wages and working conditions.[22] At about the same time the Switchmen's Union, acting alone, submitted similar demands to the railroads with which it had collective bargaining agreements.[23] The same emergency board was appointed to hear both cases and the

attempt of the board to merge the hearing in one form or another was rejected by the Switchmen's Union on the general grounds that there had already been unnecessary delay in the settlement of the dispute and any merger of issues would only prolong the settlement of the dispute.[24] It may be noted at this point, that a major factor in the refusal of the Switchmen's Union to join, either in original demands or in the hearing, with the Brotherhood of Railroad Trainmen reflected, in part, the bitterness engendered during the 1943 wage dispute and, in part, the continuous jurisdictional conflict between the two organizations. Another factor may well have been an attempt on the part of the Switchmen's Union to be the first to obtain its wage demands, and thereby obtain an advantage over the trainmen.

7. In the latter part of 1950, the Brotherhood of Locomotive Engineers and the Brotherhood of Locomotive Firemen and Enginemen each submitted separate demands for wage increases.[25] These demands were subsequently merged with the demands of the conductors and trainmen. The latter organization settled its case in 1951, while the other three did not reach agreements until 1952.

Aside from these "splits" and "conflicts" among the operating unions concerning wage demands, there has been a continuous conflict between the engineers' and firemen's unions, which has revolved chiefly around the issue of seniority. However, in recent years, there have been further sources of conflict on the question of an additional engineer or fireman on diesel locomotives. Since the line of promotion runs from fireman to engineer and since, in being promoted to engineer, a worker retains his seniority as a fireman, it is clear that in periods of declining employment engineers tend to displace firemen.[26] In addition, because the operating unions are not only agents representing workers in collective bargaining but also insurance companies, the firemen are reluctant to withdraw their membership from their original organization because of the equity in their insurance. With declining membership in both unions, the union leaders attempt to have the workers change their affiliation. This condition provides a basis for conflict. Another irritant is the question of who should be hired when an engineer's vacancy occurs—an unemployed engineer or a fireman already employed? Finally, there is a question of mileage run per day. If the engineer runs a greater mileage his pay increases, but he reduces the need for engineers and he retards the promotion of firemen. A similar type of conflict exists between the conductors and the trainmen. Although for a period of time the organizations entered into various agreements to minimize the conflict, today no such agreements exist and the "intra-organizational friction" prevails.[27] In 1949, the firemen and engineers attempted to merge their organizations. The former overwhelmingly approved the merger, but the latter rejected it.[28]

These interunion conflicts and rivalries are reflected in representation disputes brought before the National Mediation Board. In 1946, the Board pointed out that over one half of the elections conducted resulted in no change in representation. The Board added that such disputes create "friction and ill-feeling among the employees," have a "demoralizing effect on . . . the men and management," lower the "morale of the service of the transportation industry," and at times have brought on "strike threats."[29] A popular writer, in referring to this problem, has said that the operating unions are "popularly believed to be a cooperating and well-knit group of independent unions. Actually there is no group of unions in the nation more widely split or which have engaged in more serious jurisdictional battles."[30]

What is the significance of the militancy of, and the interunion rivalry among, the "operating" labor organizations? The militant attitude of the unions and of their leadership does not provide the necessary condition for stable collective bargaining between the parties, nor does it help in the settlement of disputes. The interunion rivalry and the political pressures on the union leaders for "survival and growth" also prevent prompt settlement of disputes, since the union leaders may fear that other leaders may obtain a better settlement.

In recent years another organization, an industrial type of union, has been attempting to obtain a foothold in the railroad industry with an eye toward representing all operating crafts. This organization is the United Railroad Operating Crafts, which has succeeded in winning several elections on various railroads. The main problem facing this and other organizations which attempt to establish themselves is an inability to obtain representation on the National Railroad Adjustment Board. Under the Railway Labor Act, as amended, only organizations which are national in scope can obtain a seat on the Board. The procedures for achieving this status are complex and require the determination of the Secretary of Labor. To date the United Railroad Operating Crafts has failed to obtain recognition as a "national" organization and is unable to represent its members on grievance cases before the Adjustment Board. And given the hostility of the existing railroad labor organizations toward potential rival organizations, it is not unreasonable to assume that if and when this new organization does bring cases before the Board, the representatives of the other labor organizations who are members of the board will not make an award which will help this newcomer.[31]

The Nonoperating Unions

A few of the nonoperating unions represent workers who are exclusively employed by the railroad industry. But, in general, they consist of unions whose membership includes workers engaged both in railroad and non-railroad activities. These unions, with their estimated total membership and railroad employee membership, are listed below: [32]

LABOR ORGANIZATIONS

	Total Membership	Railroad Employee Membership
Brotherhood of Railway and Steamship Clerks *et al.* (AF of L)	286,000	286,000
Brotherhood of Maintenance of Way Employees (AF of L)	150,000	150,000
International Association of Machinists (AF of L)	665,000	85,000
International Brotherhood of Boilermakers, *et al.* (AF of L)	400,000	25,000
International Brotherhood of Blacksmiths, *et al.* (AF of L)	20,000	20,000
Sheet Metal Workers International Association (AF of L)	25,000	12,000
International Brotherhood of Electrical Workers (AF of L)	313,000	12,000
Brotherhood of Railway Carmen of America (AF of L)	95,800	80,000
International Brotherhood of Firemen and Oilers (AF of L)	52,700	20,000
Brotherhood of Railroad Signalmen of America (Ind.)	13,000	13,000
Order of Railroad Telegraphers (AF of L)	55,000	50,000
National Organization of Masters, Mates, and Pilots of America (AF of L)	3,000	no report
National Marine Engineers' Beneficial Association (CIO)	11,000	no report
International Longshoremen's Association (AF of L)	61,000	no report
Hotel and Restaurant Employees International Alliance, *et al.* (AF of L)	267,000	no report
American Train Dispatchers' Association (Ind.)	3,800	3,500
Railroad Yardmasters of America (Ind.)	3,500	3,500

Although the railroad employee membership listed above adds up to about 800,000, it is generally alleged that these nonoperating unions represent about one million workers.[33]

The wage movements of the nonoperating organizations have closely paralleled those of the operating unions. However, with minor exceptions, there has been a stability in the number and types of unions participating in these wage movements, in contrast with the wage movements of the operating labor organizations. Furthermore, there has been a minimum of interunion rivalry because of the fairly sharp craft lines. Finally, in recent years this group of railroad workers has not seriously threatened a tie-up of the railroad industry, presumably because of the relatively small strategic control it has over the operations of the railroads. As was pointed out above, the problems of strikes and government seizures in the railroad industry have arisen, in recent years, more from the activities of the operating unions rather than from those of the nonoperating unions.

CHAPTER V

FEDERAL INTERVENTION IN RAILWAY LABOR DISPUTES

A STUDY of the development of railway labor legislation reveals first, that the current legislation, the Railway Labor Act, as amended in 1934, was written in light of the experience of previous railway labor legislation, the first of which was enacted in 1888; second, that the type of legislation enacted at various times in our history has reflected "economic opportunism" on the part of the unions and management; third, that each statute, after adoption, was generally hailed as *the* answer to the problem of labor disputes in the railroad industry but eventually proved unsuccessful when a serious labor dispute arose; and finally, that a serious strike or threatened strike was usually the immediate cause for the revision of the then prevailing railway labor legislation.

In the discussion of the various pieces of legislation enacted over a period of about fifty years, certain questions will be raised: Why was the legislation passed? What was the attitude of the railroads and the representatives of their employees toward the legislation? How successful was it in operation? What brought on revisions to the law? What contribution did each statute make toward the legislation now current?

THE ARBITRATION ACT OF 1888

Under the Arbitration Act of 1888 provision was made, under the law, for the adjustment of labor disputes between the railroads and their employees by two methods: voluntary arbitration and investigation.[1] Both parties could voluntarily agree to submit the dispute to a board of arbitrators consisting of three persons, one selected by each party to the dispute and a chairman agreed upon by the two. In addition, the President was authorized to appoint a temporary commission of three members to investigate the causes of any railroad labor dispute. One member of the commission, its chairman, was the United States Commissioner of Labor. Any such commission could be set up on the initiative of the President, at the request of one of the parties to the dispute, or at the request of the governor of any state.

The enactment of this first railway labor law stemmed from the serious nationwide railroad strikes of 1877, when the workers struck as a protest against reductions in wages, which in turn reflected the depressed economic conditions resulting from the panic of 1873. Although the strikes failed, the existing labor organizations "began to assume the trade union function of collective bargaining in addition to their fraternal duties." [2] During the years following, the country was gripped by "a flood of strikes" and in 1886 "the Gould railway system in the Southwest was involved in a serious struggle." [3]

Although the Arbitration Act was passed in 1888, Congress began to show an interest in legislation designed to settle disputes in the railroad industry as early as 1882. The delay in the enactment of the legislation is explained by the fact that until 1886 there were no important railway labor difficulties. Apparently, however, the strike of 1886 again precipitated interest in such legislation both on the part of Congress as well as the President.[4] Finally, in 1888 "after a series of costly and bloody railroad strikes culminating in a strike on the Chicago, Burlington and Quincy Railroad, which the federal courts sought to break through an injunction," the law was passed.[5] Another element in the passage of legislation may well have been the attitude of the legislators that, in view of the fact that the Interstate Commerce Act of 1887 gave the federal government the power to regulate the railroads, there should be some attempt to regulate the labor relations of the industry.

The railway employees favored the law while the railroads opposed it. Since "the railway labor organizations . . . were comparatively weak . . . they believed that they had nothing to lose and a possibility of gain." On the other hand, the railroads "regarded with disfavor any Government activity that would tend to interfere with the freedom of action of the managers." The railroads, however, "in theory at least, favored voluntary arbitration," but expressed "vigorous . . . opposition to compulsory arbitration." [6]

Although the Arbitration Act of 1888 was on the statute books for ten years there was not a single instance in which any labor dispute on the railroads was arbitrated, despite the fact that this provision was the cause for considerable concern and discussion.[7] The significance of the law lies in the fact that, first, it represented the first formal intervention of the federal government in the settlement of railway labor disputes; second, some of its provisions provided the basis for subsequent legislation; and, third, the investigatory provision of the law was invoked in the Pullman Strike of 1894, and although the commission which was appointed in no way took any action toward the settlement of the strike, its recommendations played a significant role in later legislation.[8] For example, the voluntary arbitration feature of the Act of 1888 still exists in our railroad labor legislation today and the use of a commission to determine the "facts" in a labor dispute is similar in many ways to the provisions of the present law with respect to the creation of emergency boards.

THE ERDMAN ACT OF 1898 [9]

The Pullman Strike of 1894 called to the attention of the public that the legislation of the time was inadequate to cope with labor disputes on the railroads.[10] From 1894 until 1898, Congress considered many bills, but it was not until June 1, 1898, that the Erdman Act was approved by the President. The new law omitted the investigatory features of the Act of 1888 but continued and strengthened the voluntary arbitration aspects of the old law. Most important, it introduced, for the first time, the policy of government mediation.

Under the law, the U.S. Commissioner of Labor and the chairman of the Interstate Commerce Commission, at the request of either party to a railway labor dispute (involving operating workers), were to make every effort to settle the dispute by mediation and conciliation. If these efforts failed, the two federal officials were to seek the arbitration of the dispute. Each side selected one arbitrator. These two, in turn, selected a neutral chairman. The latter was to be appointed by the two conciliators if agreement were not achieved by the parties within five days. The law further provided for the enforcement of all arbitrators' awards, which were to remain in effect for a period of one year. Finally, Section 10 of the law prohibited certain labor practices on the part of the employer, including discrimination against any worker because of union membership and the requirement that any worker sign a "yellow dog" contract. Part of the section of the law which was concerned with discrimination because of union membership was later declared unconstitutional.[11]

The Erdman Act of 1898 was not a "hasty and ill-advised law pushed through Congress," but rather had been carefully considered by Congress for over three years. While "the representatives of the railway labor organizations were enthusiastic in their approval of the measure," the American Federation of Labor and the railway managers reluctantly went along with the bill: the former was concerned with "the intervention of the Government in the field of labor disputes"; the latter thought that although "no good would come from the law . . . its passage was an encouraging sign of an increasing public interest in grappling with the problem of labor disturbances on the railroads." [12]

Within one year of the enactment of the law an attempt was made by one of the labor organizations to invoke mediation proceedings, but the railroads refused to participate. For more than seven years thereafter, the Act was not used as a basis for the settlement of railway labor disputes. It has been suggested that the failure to utilize the law was a reflection, in part, of the general prosperity of the period and also of prevailing public opinion, which insisted upon the peaceful settlement of railroad labor disputes.[13] After 1906, however, the provisions of the law were invoked and until the passage of the Newlands Act of 1913, a total of sixty-one cases were settled under the Erdman Act, most of them by mediation and the remainder by arbitration.[14]

Apparently, the successful operation of the law was due primarily to the personal qualities of the federal officials who administered the law and who enjoyed the confidence of both parties. But with the development of "concerted wage movements," accompanied by threatened strikes of large dimensions, there was increasing public concern over the effectiveness of the law. This state of mind brought on considerable Congressional interest, in the form of bills introduced and hearings held to amend the Erdman Act.[15]

In 1912 and 1913 the railway labor organizations initiated concerted movements for changes in their contracts. Two of the cases were settled by arbitration under the Erdman Act and a third was settled as a result of the intervention of President Wilson on the understanding that both parties would submit the controversy to arbitration if a new law were enacted.[16] Once again, strikes or threatened strikes brought forth demands for the revision of the existing laws.

It was at this time that the railroad labor organizations "realized that in a fight to the finish they had the greater strength, and they were, therefore, unwilling to have the intervention of a third party to make a decision for them which they could, perhaps, make for themselves with more gain." The railroad managers, on the other hand, now favored intervention.[17] Thus, there was a complete reversal of the attitudes of the parties since the 1880's, reflecting what has previously been referred to as "opportunism." These changed attitudes were also reflected in demands for the revision of the Erdman Act, labor asking for a freer hand, management seeking more stringent controls. A final factor causing labor distrust of the law was the decision of the Supreme Court declaring a part of Section 10 of the law unconstitutional.[18]

Probably the major contribution of the Erdman Act in the evolution of railway labor legislation was the role that mediation played in the settlement of disputes, even though it was the voluntary arbitration provision of the law which was subject to most debate prior to the enactment of the law.[19]

The Newlands Act of 1913 [20]

Recognizing that it was mediation, not arbitration, which provided the basis for the settlement of many disputes during the years preceding 1913, the Newlands Act—which has been described as simply the "Erdman Act amended and amplified" [21]—established a *permanent* Board of Mediation and Conciliation. Another significant feature of the new law was a provision for the settlement of disputes arising out of the *interpretation* of agreements, a responsibility of the same board. As was noted previously, the new law was an outgrowth of an agreement arrived at through the intervention of the President after a strike was threatened on the railroads.

After the passage of the law the services of the Board of Mediation and Conciliation were invoked frequently and it is clear that mediation, rather than arbitration, again proved to be the more important method in the settlement of labor disputes. It is significant, too, that the law apparently was successful for the first three years of operation. But by 1917, despite the sanguine hopes expressed at the time that the law was enacted, leaders of railway labor organizations were urging the virtual abolition of the Newlands Act.[22] Why this sharp change in attitude? In 1913 two railroad labor organizations initiated negotiations which culminated in the establishment of an arbitration board in 1914, at the insistence and intervention of the President, and in the issuance of an award in 1915.[23] The decision in this case was a disappointment to the employees, and their representatives voiced strong opposition to arbitration as a means for the settlement of labor disputes.[24] In other words, voluntary arbitration brought on by the pressure of the Executive, as contrasted with mediation, did not seem to be an adequate means of settling disputes.

It was this case which virtually ended the usefulness of the Newlands Act. For in 1915, the labor organizations initiated a movement for an eight-hour work day, stated that the issue was not arbitrable, and refused to refer the case for mediation. They stated that "direct negotiation between the parties was preferable to dealing through an intermediary." Again the President intervened. During negotiations a strike date was set and the workers agreed to call off the strike if the eight-hour day was enacted into law by Congress.[25] This was done, and in 1916 the Adamson Act was enacted, providing for an eight-hour work day.[26] During the controversy the President "asked Congress for compulsory arbitration legislation," but "war legislation swamped Congress before action was taken on his recommendation." [27]

In the evolution of railway labor legislation, the Newlands Act made a real contribution by establishing a permanent mediation body and by providing for a mechanism for the settlement of disputes arising out of interpretations of agreements. On the other hand, the experience under the law revealed first, that labor, recognizing its strength, was opposed to arbitration as a means of settling disputes; second, that voluntary arbitration agreed to by the parties as a result of White House pressure, does not bring about happy and peaceful solutions to labor disputes; third, that inadequate machinery for the interpretation and the enforcement of interpretations of agreements, may prove to be obstacles to the maintenance of peaceful labor relations between the parties; and fourth, that the adamant attitude of labor unions in their demands creates situations in which serious strikes are threatened and the orderly procedures for the solution of labor disputes break down. These same problems exist today.

THE ADAMSON ACT OF 1916 [28]

Although the President had made five recommendations for legislation, Congress simply provided for the establishment of an eight-hour work day and authorized the President to appoint a commission to study the effects of the eight-hour work day on the railroad industry. It turned down the suggestions of the President for an increase in the number of members of the Interstate Commerce Commission, Congressional approval of an increase in railroad rates if the eight-hour work day required it, and "an amendment to the Newlands Law making it illegal to call a strike or a lockout pending an investigation of the controversy by a Government commission." [29] It is noteworthy that this last recommendation, rejected by Congress in 1916, is now part of our present legislation.

Although the Adamson law was not concerned with procedures in the settlement of railway labor disputes, two events subsequent to the passage of the law should be noted. First, the railroads refused to institute the eight-hour work day—they claimed that the law was unconstitutional—and after a lower court so ruled, the workers threatened a strike. The issue was actually settled by mediation in 1917.[30] Second, when the law was declared constitutional by the Supreme Court in 1917, the Court asserted that Congress was using "its authority to compulsorily arbitrate the dispute." [31] This statement, which indicated that Congress had the authority to enact legislation which could require the compulsory arbitration of labor disputes, brought "joy" to the railroad managers, but consternation to the workers.[32]

FEDERAL CONTROL, 1917–1920

During the wartime period of federal control of railroads, the Railroad Administration developed "certain principles, policies and methods . . . for overcoming the weaknesses of mediation and arbitration as they appeared under the Newlands Act." [33] The workers were not to be discriminated against for membership in unions and this right resulted in considerable growth in the membership of the railroad labor organizations. In addition, the director general entered into *national* agreements with the labor organizations. Finally, railway boards of adjustment were created to handle grievances arising out of the interpretation of collective bargaining agreements, if any such disputes arose.

"The orders, policies, and practices of the Railroad Administration laid the basis for many of the provisions later embodied in the Railway Labor Act." [34] Although it has been alleged that labor was "pampered" during this period, "the fact remains that during the Federal control of railroads, labor difficulties on the roads were at a minimum." [35] Whether this labor peace was due to federal control or to the fact that the country was at war is uncertain. But apparently railroad labor was satisfied with the intervention of the government.[36]

TRANSPORTATION ACT OF 1920 [37]

When the railroads were returned to private ownership after the war, there was considerable Congressional activity directed toward the amendment of the Newlands Act of 1913.[38] There was, however, disagreement over how the law should be changed. For example, the Senate enacted a bill providing for compulsory arbitration, but the House rejected it.[39] The law which finally emerged "represented compromises and accommodations of many views" and "the provisions . . . were vague in their purposes, capable of a multiplicity of interpretations, and uncertain in their legal authority." [40] Basically, the law provided two things with respect to railroad labor: that both parties make every effort to settle their disputes themselves and that unresolved disputes be referred to the United States Railroad Labor Board, which the statute created, for "hearing and decision." The law provided, in addition, for the establishment of adjustment boards on the basis of agreement between the parties.

Immediately after the enactment of the law, both parties indicated that they would utilize fully the procedures under the law, although it was passed over labor's opposition.[41] Labor supported the Plumb Plan, which provided for the continued operation of the railroads by the government, thereby reflecting their pleasure over the administration of the director general during the period of federal control.[42]

Most students of the problem agree that the legislation under which the Railroad Labor Board functioned failed in its objectives.[43] The basic cause, according to one writer, was the fact that the railroads were unwilling to accept the gains the unions had made during the war and "the unions refused to relinquish them without a struggle." [44]

Administratively, the Railroad Labor Board was swamped with adjustment cases and had no power to enforce its decisions. (This problem was to reappear later.) In addition, the Board was carrying out both mediation and arbitration functions—which displeased both groups.[45]

Labor was severely critical of the Board. It felt that the chairman was hostile;[46] under the decisions of the Board the shopmen's strike of 1922 was broken and company unions virtually encouraged, resulting in a rapid growth of such unions within a period of four months; [47] the Board gave inadequate consideration to the principle of a "living wage" and too much consideration to the principle of "ability to pay"; [48] labor thought the right of the Board to determine wages and working rules limited the right of collective bargaining; [49] and, the workers were dissatisfied with long delays involved in the decision-making process of the Board.[50] The law became completely ineffective when the Supreme Court rejected a union's application for the enforcement of a decision of the Railroad Labor Board which directed a railroad to deal with a regular labor union rather than a company-dominated union.[51]

Despite the fact that the Railroad Labor Board, in its first five years of existence, handled about 13,000 disputes, that during this period the number of serious strikes was small, and aside from the fact that most of the Board's decisions were carried out, the law was eventually discredited for the reasons cited above.[52]

Although very few of the law's provisions have proved useful today, the experiences derived from the operations under the statute can be of help. This experience demonstrates: (1) that the mediation and arbitration functions need to be separated; (2) that governmental determination of wages and working conditions must be avoided; [53] (3) that mediation—which the law failed to provide for—had proved to be the best method up to that time; (4) that both sides to a dispute must be willing to cooperate under the law; (5) that the so-called adjustment work should be separated from other activities or else it would overwhelm the operations of the Board in settling broader issues of collective bargaining.

THE RAILWAY LABOR ACT OF 1926 [54]

From the time of the enactment of the Transportation Act of 1920 until 1926, there was considerable Congressional activity in an attempt to revise the procedures for settling railway labor disputes.[55] In 1926, railway labor and management, after a series of compromises, jointly agreed to arrangements which duly became embodied in the Railway Labor Act.[56] It has been asserted that this law "embodies all the devices of the earlier statutes except the quasi-judicial, but impotent, Labor Board." [57] Adjustment boards, for the settlement of disputes arising out of existing contracts, were to be established by agreement between the parties. Each agreement for the establishment of an adjustment board was to provide that disputes between an employee, or group of employees, and a carrier, growing out of grievances or out of the interpretation or application of agreements concerning rates of pay, rules, or working conditions, should be handled in the usual manner up to and including the chief operating officer of the carrier designated to handle such disputes. If the parties fail to reach an adjustment in this manner, the dispute was to be referred to a designated adjustment board by the parties, or by either party, with a full statement of the facts and all supporting data bearing on the dispute. Furthermore, the agreement was to "stipulate that decisions of adjustment boards shall be final and binding on both parties to the dispute; and it shall be the duty of both to abide by such decisions."

A Board of Mediation, similar to that operating under the Erdman and Newlands Acts, and consisting of five members, was created. The law provided that

the parties, or either party, to a dispute between an employee or group of employees and a carrier may invoke the services of the Board of Mediation . . . or the Board of Mediation can proffer its services, in any of the following cases:

(a) A dispute arising out of grievances or out of the interpretation or application of agreements concerning rates of pay, rules, or working conditions not adjusted by the parties in conference and not decided by the appropriate adjustment board;

(b) A dispute which is not settled in conference between the parties, in respect to changes in rates of pay, rules, or working conditions;

(c) Any other dispute not decided in conference between the parties.

It should be noted that the Board could intervene in grievance cases only if all of the procedures are followed and could not intervene directly on its own accord.

The 1926 law stated further that if the Board were unsuccessful in its mediation efforts it should make every effort to induce both sides to submit the controversy to arbitration. The procedure for the arbitration of disputes was carefully spelled out in the law, presumably because it was expected that this method would prove to be most useful in the settlement of labor disputes.

Finally, the law provided for the appointment of emergency boards by the President to investigate all disputes and report to the President. After the creation of such a board, and for thirty days after the issuance of the board's report, "no change, except by agreement, shall be made by the parties to the controversy in the conditions out of which the dispute arose." This in effect meant "no strike" during this period. This procedure for the "investigation" of the dispute is similar, to a marked degree, to the provisions of the law of 1888. It should be noted that the law does not specifically require an emergency board to make recommendations, nor does it make any reference to "fact-finding" on the part of the board. Yet, the practice has been for the boards to "find facts" and make recommendations. The significant feature of this law, according to one student of labor, was "the underlying idea . . . that the railroads and their employees can best settle their own troubles and that government ought to intervene only when they fail." [58]

Again, this law was greeted with a great deal of optimism by both sides.[59] Writing in 1931, one writer stated that "this act has now been in effect for four years and has apparently worked well. While no one can predict what the future will bring, we seemingly have devised the best method of dealing with railroad labor disputes yet devised." [60] Another writer in 1933 stated that "the effectiveness of the Railway Labor Act is evidenced by the fact that during the six and one-half years of its history, despite 29 strike ballots among railway employees, only two insignificant strikes have occurred." [61]

Despite the basic agreement between labor and management in the writing of the law and despite the optimism of students of the problem, the railroad unions, according to a report of the Twentieth Century Fund, still were dissatisfied, while the carriers "found it almost entirely satisfactory." [62] Why did labor change its attitude? First, the railroads were continuing certain practices which were presumably prohibited under the Railway Labor Act, e.g., the sponsorship of company-dominated unions. Second, few adjustment boards were established, chiefly "because of the carriers' aversion to national agreements." This meant that disputes arising out of the interpretation of agreements could not be settled since the Board of Mediation could intervene only upon the request of one of the parties and only on the basis of an appeal from a decision of an adjustment board. Third, these adjustment boards, when established, were frequently deadlocked over the issues and there was no recourse to an impartial person.

Despite this dissatisfaction on the part of railroad labor, the strikes during this period were few in number and insignificant. But this fact does not necessarily reflect effectiveness in the operation of the Railway Labor Act of 1926. The serious financial condition of the railroads during the depression surely must have softened the demands of railroad labor and played a role in the labor peace of the period under discussion. In fact, in 1932, the railroad unions voluntarily accepted a wage cut.[63] In addition, the wages of railroad workers, as a group, had declined less after 1929 than those of other industrial workers.[64]

As a result of pressure on the part of both the railway labor organizations and the Federal Coordinator of Transportation, amendments to the Railway Labor Act were enacted in 1934. However, except for certain specific amendments described below, "the Railway Labor Act remains [today], in its essentials, the same as it was enacted in 1926." [65]

Amendments to the Bankruptcy and Emergency Transportation Acts, 1933

Early in 1933, Congress, in amending the Bankruptcy Act,[66] provided that carriers managed by trustees or courts (1) should not change wages or working conditions except in accordance with the provisions of the existing law or in accordance with the 1932 wage reduction agreement; (2) were prohibited from influencing employees in the joining of labor organizations and from dominating any union; and (3) were prohibited from requiring employees to sign "yellow dog" contracts. Subsequently, under the Emergency Railroad Transportation Act of 1933, these provisions were made applicable to *all* carriers.[67]

These prohibitions reflected the experience under the Railway Labor Act of 1926. In 1930, the Supreme Court, in effect, disestablished a company-dominated union, a type of union which had not been completely stamped out under the 1926 law.[68] This decision, plus the prohibitions noted above, provided the basis for the 1934 amendments to the Railway Labor Act.

THE 1934 AMENDMENTS [69]

In 1934 the Railway Labor Act of 1926 was amended. It not only incorporated the labor provisions of the emergency laws of 1933 but also attempted to improve the 1926 law in those areas in which it was found to be deficient.

First, the amendments prohibited the carriers from resorting to certain labor practices. The carriers, for example, were directed to bargain collectively with the representatives of the workers and were not in any way to "interfere with, influence, or coerce" the workers in their choice of representatives. In addition, the carriers were barred from utilizing the "yellow dog" contract in the employment of railroad workers. Finally, the carriers were not in any way to interfere with the right of the workers to select their own organization for the purpose of collective bargaining—in effect, company-sponsored unions were barred.

Second, the law provided for the establishment of a permanent, bipartisan National Board of Adjustment, to which disputes arising out of the interpretation and application of collective bargaining agreements might be submitted by either party.[70] To eliminate the many deadlocked cases which frequently arose under the operation of the 1926 law, provision was made for the appointment of referees in such situations. Furthermore, if the carrier failed to comply with the award of the Board, the petitioner had the right to seek enforcement of the order in the courts.

Third, the 1934 amendments established a new Board of Mediation, consisting of three members. Their powers and responsibilities were similar in many respects to those of the 1926 law. However, the Board was empowered to proffer its services in *any* dispute which might result in a "labor emergency."

Fourth, the Board was empowered to conduct representation elections for the purpose of determining the bargaining representatives of the employees.

Finally, the law made the closed shop illegal, in an attempt to eliminate the company-unions which had grown up over the years.[71]

The amendments of 1934 were the last significant changes in the railway labor legislation of this country. Subsequent to their enactment, and prior to the outbreak of World War II, many students of labor and various public officials extolled the virtues of the law under which the railroads and their workers were governed. One student, writing apparently in 1941 and pointing to "the long period of unbroken peace on the railroads," states that the success of the Railway Labor Act, as amended, can be ascribed to the sensitivity of both parties to public opinion, "the maturity of the industry and that of the organizations . . . ," and the fact that the employees have "fared well," compared with other industrial workers, "without having to resort to the inconvenience and expense of strikes." [72] Another writer points out that, despite certain flaws, "the National Mediation Board is the best contemporary example of a successful mediation agency. The law is in general, well-conceived and effectively administered." [73]

The former Secretary of Labor, Frances Perkins, made glowing references to the administration of the railway labor law and President Truman referred to it as a "model" to be used in enacting legislation to curb strikes in other industries.[74] The National Mediation Board, after one year of operation, pointed out that the "principles and methods" for settling labor disputes, as set forth in the Railway Labor Act, "provide a model labor policy, based on equal rights and equitable relations." [75]

To what extent has this optimism been justified? Once again, as in earlier periods of our history, there is today considerable concern over the effectiveness of the present railway labor legislation. The number of strikes in the railroad industry—and their size—has been steadily increasing since 1940.[76] During the past decade, the federal government has seized the railroads a number of times because either a strike was threatened or a strike was in process.[77] The National Mediation Board in 1951 reports that it "is . . . disturbed by the apparent reluctance of both the carriers and the organizations, in national cases, to conduct thorough collective bargaining." The Board is also concerned about a "breakdown" in the operation of the National Railroad Adjustment Board. The Board reports further that "mediation of these national wage and rules movements has, in most cases, proved unsuccessful" and there is a tendency on the part of the employees to reject the recommendations of the emergency boards established under the law.[78] In 1951 the Senate Committee on Labor and Public Welfare conducted hearings to study the operations of the Railway Labor Act and to make such recommendations as were necessary to solve the many problems that existed. The report of the Committee indicated a need for the revision of the existing legislation.[79]

The history of railway labor legislation, summarized above, seems to warrant the following conclusions:

First, that the most successful method for the settling of railway labor disputes has been mediation. Voluntary arbitration, resulting from the coercion by the office of the President, was seldom successful.

Second, that the railroad labor organizations and the carriers have consistently acted in an opportunistic manner, supporting or attacking legislation simply in terms of benefits to be derived from the law.

Third, that in most instances the serious strikes which brought about demands for new legislation arose out of the economic conditions of the period and did not necessarily arise simply out of the defects of the legislation designed to handle the disputes.

Fourth, that either inadequate machinery for the settlement of grievances or lack of power to enforce decisions on grievance disputes brought about serious difficulties.

If these conclusions from history are borne in mind, one can have a better understanding of the current railway labor problem and a better insight into its solution. It might be suggested at this point that the solution to the problem will not necessarily come from improved legislation, but rather from some rapport between the parties involved.[80]

Part II: The Railway Labor Act in Operation

CHAPTER VI

THE RAILWAY LABOR ACT: SUCCESS OR FAILURE?

IN 1937, Secretary of Labor, Frances Perkins, testifying before a Congressional Committee stated that "the Railway Labor Act embodies the fullest and most complete development of mediation, conciliation, voluntary agreement, and arbitration that is to be found in any law governing labor relations," and that the "administration of the Railway Labor Act . . . is an outstanding example of effective administration of a labor law." [1]

Yet in 1951, Senator Wayne L. Morse, at a meeting of the Senate Committee on Labor and Public Welfare is reported to have said that the National Mediation Board was "a window-dressing institution that accomplishes no good" in the settlement of labor disputes in the railroad industry. Senator Morse asserted, further, that he did not think "we can justify keeping on the books much longer a board that costs the taxpayers so many thousands of dollars and has a record of so many failures." [2]

Similarly, in 1941 a student of railroad labor legislation, Harry D. Wolf, in his appraisal of the operations of the Railway Labor Act, stated that if the "fundamental purposes [of collective bargaining] are to promote friendly discussion and to substitute negotiations for the strike and lock-out in settling differences between employers and employees . . . the results [under the Railway Labor Act] must be regarded as highly successful." [3] On the other hand, another student of railroad labor legislation has noted that since 1941 labor disputes involving national unions and the entire railroad industry have resulted in "union repudiation of emergency board decisions, threatened or actual strikes, and usually government seizure." [4] This same observer stated elsewhere that "the Railway Labor Act, far from being a 'model' law, should be thoroughly recast," and concluded that "the emergency board procedure has actually retarded both collective bargaining and the use of voluntary arbitration machinery." [5]

Finally, in reporting to Congress in 1939, the National Mediation Board noted with apparent satisfaction that the railroad industry's operations were not interrupted because of labor difficulties in 1939 and pointed out that "the people of the country, their industry, business, and commerce, have been able to count on reliable, safe, and efficient transportation service free from interruptions due to labor troubles, all as contemplated by the Railway Labor Act." [6] In 1950, in a similar report to Congress, the same Board noted that "during the year, the number of threatened strikes in the transportation industry was greater than in any previous year of the life of the act." [7] The whole tone of the report is one of serious concern over the more recent developments in collective bargaining relationships in the railroad industry.[8]

How does one account for the changes in attitudes of government officials, students of the labor movement, and government bodies? Were the experts of over a decade ago right or wrong? Are the present critics right or wrong? What condition arose during the past ten or fifteen years which may indicate that the early optimists and the present skeptics are both correct? Are there inherent defects in the Railway Labor Act which have not—for good reasons—become apparent until recent years?

In the following chapters the writer will attempt to indicate that:

1. Although the so-called "over-all" record of the activities of the National Mediation Board seems impressive, a careful analysis does not support this impression.
2. The major reasons for the breakdown of collective bargain-

ing as a result of the administration of the Railway Labor Act are:

a) The deterioration of the relative wage position of the railroad workers. This deterioration is a reflection of the fact that the emergency boards have failed to employ uniform, consistent, and objective standards for wage determinations. If such standards had been employed, the railroad workers would probably have kept pace with other comparable groups of workers.

b) The establishment of the principle of compulsory arbitration—*de facto* but not *de jure*—for the settlement of disputes arising out of changes in the rates of pay, rules, and working conditions in the railroad industry. This situation came about as a result of the intervention of the President and the courts in railroad labor disputes.

c) The breakdown of the grievance procedure, including the procedure followed by the National Railroad Adjustment Board, particularly the division of the Board concerned with the grievances of the operating workers.

d) The existence of certain inherent defects in the Railway Labor Act, as amended, either in its provisions or in the procedures established under it.

Two points should be emphasized. First, that the abovementioned reasons for the breakdown of collective bargaining in the railroad industry stem from the administration of and operations under the Railway Labor Act. Other factors contributing to this breakdown, including the financial situation of the railroads, the recent mechanization program of the railroads, declining employment opportunities within the industry, and the elaborate and complex working rules, are also significant in this regard and have been discussed in the preceding chapters. Second, that all of these factors have played interdependent roles in the breakdown of collective bargaining. For example, there is an interconnection between the financial condition of the railroads, the problem of working rules, and the breakdown of the grievance machinery. Similarly, the very existence of *de facto* compulsory arbitration may have influenced the findings of the emergency boards and may have also been an important element in the breakdown of the grievance machinery.

CHAPTER VII

THE RECORD: 1934-1952

IN THE APPRAISAL of the operations of the Railway Labor Act two assertions are usually made: first, that the number and extent of strikes in the railroad industry have been substantially less than in all other industries; and, second, that over the years about 72 percent of all labor disputes brought before the National Mediation Board have been settled constructively "through the three avenues of mediation agreement, arbitration agreement, and withdrawals during or after mediation."[1] These assertions seem to indicate that the administration of the Railway Labor Act has been successful. An analysis of the data on the basis of which these statements are made reveals, however, that opposite conclusions may be drawn.

STRIKES IN THE RAILROAD INDUSTRY

From 1934 to 1952, the number and extent of the strikes in the railroad industry have increased. In 1952 there were seventeen work stoppages, as compared with twenty-four strikes during the fiscal year 1951.[2] The decline from 1951 to 1952 reflects the fact that the railroads were under Army control for eleven months of the fiscal year 1952.[3] Since the railroads were returned to private management in May of 1952 and with the removal of the power of the President of the United States to seize the transportation system of the country under a 1916 statute, strikes and threatened strikes continue.

It was the unusual strike picture of the 1930's—in contrast with other industries—which created the impression of a "model" railway labor law, at least during that decade. But

TABLE 2

WORK STOPPAGES IN THE RAILROAD INDUSTRY, 1934-1949

Year	Number of Stoppages	Number of Workers Involved	MAN-DAYS IDLE	
			Number	Percent of Working Time
1934	0	0	0	.0
1935	1	30	60	a
1936	2	590	22,900	a
1937	6	1,100	26,400	a
1938	1	30	130	a
1939	0	0	0	.0
1940	1	70	570	a
1941	5	1,160	22,200	a
1942	9	1,340	17,500	a
1943	8	3,270	9,230	a
1944	12	3,240	25,600	a
1945	13	5,790	56,900	.01
1946	15	356,000	912,000	.20
1947	7	13,900	288,000	.06
1948	12	3,670	108,000	.02
1949	10	49,700	1,180,000	.31

a Less than 1/100 of 1 percent.

Source: *Sixteenth Annual Report of the National Mediation Board*, p. 6.

such a conclusion failed to take into account the fact that the railroad unions during this period were fairly well established, their organizing drives were at a minimum, and collective bargaining relationships had been established. These conditions did not exist in other industries where many strikes arose primarily over the question of recognition and where collective bargaining was in its infancy.[4]

Another factor which explains the unusual quietude in the railroad industry during the 1930's was the generally depressed economic conditions of the period. Actually, during this period, the railroad unions had agreed to a wage *cut* of 10 percent, effective February 1, 1932, for a period of one year. This agreement was extended twice to June 30, 1934, at which time 2½ percent of the deduction was restored. Subsequently, "on January 1, 1935, an additional 2½ percent was restored, and the remaining 5 percent was restored on April 1, 1935." [5]

This reduction in wages resulted in a decrease in average hourly *earnings* of about 5 cents: from 65 cents an hour to 60 cents an hour. From 1929 to 1932—the first year of the wage reduction—the average hourly earnings of railroad workers were not only higher than those of all workers in manufacturing industries but fell less than the latter group: from 64 cents an hour to 60 cents an hour, in contrast to a drop of from 57 cents an hour to 45 cents an hour for workers in manufacturing industries. Although after 1932 the wages of workers in manufacturing industries increased more than the wages of workers in the railroad industry, the average hourly earnings of the former were still less than those of the latter until 1942, the first year in which the average factory worker received higher average hourly earnings than the railroad worker. And this superiority continues to date.[6] These wage relationships during the period of a depression may also explain why the strikes in the thirties were rare in the railroad industry.

It has been pointed out, however, that even during the past ten years, when organization drives in other industries have slowed down and when collective bargaining relationships were on a fairly stable basis, the incidence of the strikes— measured in estimated working time lost—has been consistently less serious in the railroad industry than in all industries combined.[7] To what extent can one infer from these data that collective bargaining has been relatively more stable in the railroad industry than in all other industries? In the first place, it is suggested that the comparisons are not necessarily valid. The railroad industry is all but completely organized while "all other industries" are not, and it is not unreasonable to assume that the incidence of strikes is lower in unorganized industries.[8] Second, the data include actual strikes and do not consider *threatened* strikes, which in the past few years have become serious in the railroad industry. For example, in the face of threatened strikes the railroads were taken over by the government in 1943 before any strike could actually take place;[9] this threatened strike would not appear in the strike data, but would be indicative of the status of labor relations in the industry. The National Mediation Board reported that during the fiscal year ended June 30, 1950, "the number of threatened strikes in the transportation industry was greater than in any previous year of the life of the act."[10] Of course, the threat of a strike "does not necessarily mean that a strike is seriously contemplated," as was pointed out by one writer.[11] What is suggested here is that data on actual strikes and their extent in the railroad industry are not an exact test of the degree of success of the railway labor law nor of the stability of collective bargaining relationships under it.[12]

Finally, a study of the unions involved in work stoppages in the railroad industry since 1941 indicates that in most instances the unions involved belonged to the operating group and that the important strikes—measured in terms of the number of workers involved—were called by unions belonging to this same group.[13] Furthermore, the seizures of the railroads in recent years on the part of the federal government have usually followed strikes or threatened strikes by the operating unions. This would seem to indicate that the more important railroad unions—measured not in terms of membership but in terms of the strategic role they play in the operations of the railroads—have not been utilizing the procedures of the Railway Labor Act as was originally intended.

The incidence of strikes and threatened strikes among this group of railroad workers might not compare favorably with the rest of the industry.

Although nothing written above demonstrates conclusively that the Railway Labor Act has failed to bring industrial peace to the railroad industry, it does demonstrate that only the careless use of strike data proves the contrary.

MEDIATION ACTIVITIES IN THE RAILROAD INDUSTRY

During the eighteen years ending June 30, 1952, the National Mediation Board handled a total of 4,043 cases involving mediation of disputes in the railroad industry and, in one way or another, disposed of a total of 3,910 cases.[14] How were these cases handled? How many were settled? According to the report of the National Mediation Board, the 3,910 cases were handled and disposed of as follows:

Cases	Number	Percent of Total
Mediation agreements	2,073	53.0
Arbitration agreements	150	3.8
Withdrawn after mediation	596	15.3
Withdrawn before mediation	360	9.2
Refusal to arbitrate	662	16.9
Dismissal	69	1.8
Total	3,910	100.0

It can be seen from the above figures that voluntary arbitration, a method which it was hoped would be utilized by both parties in the settlement of railway labor disputes, has played a minor role. And the number of disputes settled in this manner has been declining in the past few years. Although over two thousand mediation agreements have been obtained through the intervention of the Board, it is pertinent to inquire as to the seriousness of the issues involved and the number of workers involved in these disputes. A special study covering the period 1934–1950, made by the National Mediation Board, reveals the following with respect to the issues involved in these mediation agreements: [15]

Issues Involved	Number of Cases	Percent of Total
Negotiation of new agreements	221	12.3
Changes in rates of pay	572	31.8
Changes and revisions in rules	901	50.0
Miscellaneous	106	5.9
Total	1,800	100.0

The above figures indicate that changes in working rules and in rates of pay have been the two principal issues involved in mediation cases. These requested changes, however, which have been successfully mediated usually arise "after the major issues have been disposed of" and it is to be expected that they would be settled.[16] Apparently, too, the mediation has not involved large groups of workers, for the Board points out that "during the past several years, the number of complete revisions of individual working agreements on the rail carriers has greatly diminished, since the trend now is toward major rules revisions through the medium of national wage and rules movements." [17] It has been noted that

in an industry like the railroads where national collective bargaining settles basic wage issues, it would be surprising indeed if most of the cases requiring government intervention were not settled by mediation. Hence, the fact that mediation is used more than any other form of government intervention does not mean that it is either the most satisfactory or the most successful, but rather that it is the method most useful for minor controversies when the major issues have been disposed of.[18]

The evidence on the mediation activities of the National Mediation Board would seem to indicate that major issues in critical cases have not been settled by mediation since the passage of the amendments to the Railway Labor Act in 1934. These important cases have involved nationwide or concerted wages and rules movements and the methods employed in handling these disputes are described below.

NATIONAL WAGE AND RULES MOVEMENTS

Since 1934 only two cases involving large groups of railroad workers were settled by mediation. Two additional cases were resolved by the submission of the issues to arbitration boards, but the railroad labor organizations were so dissatisfied with the awards that they immediately submitted new demands for wage increases. The remainder of the movements were finally settled through White House intervention in one form or another, after all the procedures under the Railway Labor Act had been exhausted.

In 1937 agreement was reached by mediation for increasing the wages of both the operating and nonoperating workers.[19]

In 1938 the railroads notified the workers that they intended to reduce wage rates by 15 percent. Attempts to settle the case by mediation or voluntary arbitration failed, and eventually the President appointed an emergency board, in conformance with the Railway Labor Act, which concluded that "no horizontal reduction upon a national scale of the wages of railway labor should be pressed by the carriers at this time."[20] The carriers accepted the recommendations of the board.

In 1941 both the operating and nonoperating groups initiated wage and rule movements. Again mediation failed and voluntary arbitration was not accepted. After a strike vote was taken, the President appointed an emergency board. The recommendations of the board were accepted by the carriers, but rejected by the labor organizations.[21] The case was then taken up by the President who, after discussions with the interested parties, reconvened the board "for the purpose of giving the parties an opportunity to reargue the case by stating their exceptions and objections to the Board's recommendations and by presenting any new evidence which they might wish to offer."[22] After reargument, the Board offered its services for mediation, which were accepted and provided the basis for the settlement of the issue.[23] It is to be noted that the procedures for reargument and mediation followed in this case went beyond the procedures of the law, and the unions obtained more than was originally recommended by the emergency board.

In late 1942 the nonoperating group, and in early 1943 the operating group, asked for higher wages. Again mediation was unsuccessful. Eventually, in 1943, an emergency board investigating the nonoperating-group demands, recommended certain wage increases which were subsequently disapproved by the Economic Stabilization Director.[24] According to Northrup, an attempt was made by the latter official to reconvene the board, but the chairman refused. Thereupon, the President appointed a new emergency board "pursuant to his war powers" and not under the provisions of the Railway Labor Act.[25] Again, the unions rejected the board's recommendations which were in conformance with the standards established by the Economic Stabilization Director.

While these events were taking place, the operating group's case was heard by another emergency board whose recommendations were also rejected by the unions.[26] A threatened strike by the operating group brought a suggestion by the President that he arbitrate the dispute. Railroad management and two of the unions—the engineers and the trainmen—accepted, but the other three operating unions refused; whereupon the President seized the railroads.[27] The President's arbitration award for the two operating unions provided the basis for the settlement of the cases involving the other operating unions and the nonoperating group.[28] Once again, the unions obtained more than what was originally recommended by the emergency boards.

In mid-1946, all of the unions demanded wage increases and changes in the rules. The nonoperating group and three operating unions—the firemen, conductors, and switchmen—agreed to arbitrate. The engineers and trainmen refused to arbitrate, and an emergency board was established. The hearings before the two arbitration boards and the emergency board were conducted separately, but simultaneously. The three boards recommended the same wage increase—sixteen cents an hour.[29] Although the two groups which agreed to arbitration had to accept the recommendations to avoid being accused of "bad faith," they immediately made further demands for a wage increase, indicating their dissatisfaction with the awards. The engineers and trainmen rejected the recommendations of the emergency board. The latter group rejected an offer made by the President—in excess of the emergency board's recommendations—and went on strike, *after* the President seized the railroads.[30] The strike was called off when the President requested drastic legislation from Congress. Settlement was finally based on the President's original offer.[31] The other two groups, the nonoperating and the three operating unions, settled their "additional" demands on the same basis.

In 1947 the nonoperating unions and the operating unions initiated separate wage movements. The former group agreed to arbitration, accepted the award, and the case was disposed of.[32] The trainmen and conductors settled their dispute as a result of mediation, but the other three operating unions, after threatening to strike, presented their case to an emergency board in 1948.[33] The recommendations of the board were accepted by the railroads, but rejected by the unions. After fruitless discussions with the National Mediation Board and the President, and after a strike date was set, the government seized the railroads and the Secretary of the Army obtained a temporary injunction from the Court which forbade any strike action.[34] Further conferences resulted in the final termination of the dispute.[35]

In 1948, the demands of the five operating unions for a wage increase were satisfactorily disposed of by mediation while the requests of the nonoperating unions for a forty-hour work week, as well as a wage increase, were disposed of after the parties accepted the recommendations of the emergency board. In the first case, the settlement was based on a wage pattern which had been established in other industries.[36] In the second case the nonoperating unions obtained their demand for a forty-hour work week, with the maintenance of take-home pay, plus a wage increase.[37]

In 1949 the Brotherhood of Railroad Trainmen and the Order of Railway Conductors jointly presented demands for a reduction in hours, including a forty-hour work week with maintenance of take-home pay for yard workers, and certain wage increases. During the same period the Switchmen's Union filed a similar request with the carriers. After considerable delay and unsuccessful negotiations, an emergency board was established. Its recommendations, issued in 1950, were rejected by the operating unions.[38] The Switchmen's Union, after calling off a threatened strike, finally struck five railroads. After two weeks, the union called off its strike against four of the carriers. The President then seized the one railroad, but the strike continued until a temporary injunction was issued by the District Court.[39] This case was settled later when the railroads offered somewhat more than what was recommended by the emergency board. Mediation efforts continued with respect to the other two operating unions with no success. In August, 1950, the President ordered the seizure of the railroads when the two unions threatened a strike.[40] A temporary restraining order was issued by the District Court on December 14, 1950, after which discussions were continued in the White House until an agreement was signed on December 21, 1950.[41] However, the general chairmen of the unions, to whom the agreement was submitted for approval, rejected the agreement.[42] The agreement covered not only the wage and hour demands of the trainmen and conductors, but also the engineers and the firemen who had submitted wage and hour demands in the fall of 1950. The rejection of the agreement resulted in cries of "bad faith." In March, 1951, the trainmen were held in contempt of court for violation of an injunction because a small number of yardmen left their jobs because of "sickness." [43]

While the negotiations of the operating unions were going on, the nonoperating group asked for a wage increase in October, 1950. This case was settled by mediation—with the intervention of the White House—on March 1, 1951, the settlement following the pattern set by the Wage Stabilization Board.[44] One of the operating unions, the Brotherhood of Railroad Trainmen, finally settled its case in May, 1951, virtually on the basis of the December 21, 1950, agreement.[45] The other three operating unions—conductors, firemen, and engineers—concluded their agreements on May 23, 1952.[46]

From this description of negotiation for contract changes on a nationwide basis, certain facts stand out:
1. Since 1941 the procedures followed in the settlement of railway labor disputes arising out of contract changes have extended beyond those provided for in the Railway Labor Act, as amended, in the form of White House intervention, court injunction, and government seizure.
2. In the few instances where mediation was successful, the unions received wage increases which were equal to those being received by workers in other industries.
3. When the unions thought that what was being offered to them in the form of a wage increase was either less than that being offered to workers in other industries, or insufficient to eliminate certain wage inequities, a strike or

threatened strike, followed by the intervention of the President, usually yielded more than that recommended by the emergency boards.

4. In the most recent cases, the unions, particularly the operating unions, have indicated continuous dissatisfaction with the wage recommendations, even after Presidential intervention.

It would seem, on the basis of the record, that the railroad labor organizations have been dissatisfied with the wage recommendations of the emergency boards and the President during the past decade. Is there any basis for this dissatisfaction? To what extent has this group of workers suffered any deterioration in their economic position? These questions will be discussed in the following chapter.

CHAPTER VIII

THE EARNINGS POSITION OF RAILROAD WORKERS

A STUDENT of labor has asserted that the railroad workers who were once "the aristocrats of labor . . . had developed . . . considerable dissatisfaction . . . over the deterioration of their relative earning status." [1] If this is so—and the analysis below will support this conclusion—two questions might be asked: What were the causes for this deterioration, and is it necessarily "bad" from an equitable point of view? It is not the intention of the writer to answer the second question at this point because, aside from the problem of making a judgment of this type, it is sufficient to indicate simply that the fact that the wage position of these workers has deteriorated may well explain the insufficiencies of collective bargaining in the railroad industry. The second question will be discussed in Chapter IX.

One problem which arises in the comparison of the changing wage positions of different groups of workers is the base date to be used. Since this study is concerned primarily with the years after 1934, it would at first seem obvious that this year be considered as the base date. But in 1934 the railroad workers had voluntarily agreed to a wage cut, and it was not until 1936 that their original wage was completely restored. Therefore, 1936 will be used as a base date.

It is important, too, to break down the earnings of railroad workers into two groups—the operating and nonoperating—to determine whether or not there are any significant differences in the changes in their relative earning status which may explain, in part, differences in the militancy of the two groups.

In Table 3 are given the average hourly earnings of workers in manufacturing industries and of all railroad workers since 1936. On the basis of these data the railroads and the railroad labor organizations come to different conclusions.

TABLE 3

AVERAGE HOURLY EARNINGS, WORKERS IN MANUFACTURING INDUSTRIES AND THE RAILROAD INDUSTRY, 1936–1952
(Cents per Hour)

Year	Manufacturing Workers	Railroad Workers
1936	55.6	65.9
1937	62.4	67.6
1938	62.7	71.2
1939	63.3	71.4
1940	66.1	71.7
1941	72.9	75.1
1942	85.3	82.4
1943	96.1	89.7
1944	101.9	93.8
1945	102.3	94.2
1946	108.6	111.6
1947	123.7	117.0
1948	135.0	130.9
1949	140.1	141.9
1950	146.5	154.9
1951	159.4	170.2
1952 (Dec.)	173.2	189.9

Sources: For manufacturing workers: United States Department of Labor, *Handbook of Labor Statistics*, 1950 ed., pp. 58, 59; *Monthly Labor Review*, January, 1953, pp. 87, 102; and *Hours and Earnings*, February, 1953, p. 3. For railroad workers: *The Economic Report of the President*, January, 1953, p. 180, and I.C.C. Statement No. M-300, December, 1952.

The railroads, on the one hand, assert that the data reveal that over the years the railroad workers have improved themselves relative to workers in manufacturing industries. The labor organizations argue, on the other hand, that further analysis of the data reveal the contrary.

The railroads point to the fact that from 1936 to the end of the year 1952 the average hourly earnings of railroad workers increased $1.24, as compared with $1.18 for workers in manufacturing industries. They assert that the wage differential has spread from ten cents an hour in favor of railroad workers in 1936 to seventeen cents an hour in favor of railroad workers at the end of 1952.[2]

The labor organizations, in rebuttal, have essentially three arguments.[3] First, they say that about twenty-three cents of the increase since 1936 reflects the changeover from a forty-eight-hour to a forty-hour work week for nonoperating workers, which went into effect in September, 1949. This change in the length of the work week did not result in any increase in take-home pay and did not materially affect the weekly or annual earnings of the railroad workers. The labor organizations note that workers in manufacturing industries had by 1936 already changed over to a shorter work week.

Second, according to the labor organizations, the proper criterion is not money wages but rather real wages, that is, the money wages adjusted for changes in the cost of living. On the basis of this adjustment the labor organizations argue that real wages of railroad workers increased by thirty-four cents an hour from 1936 to the end of 1952, while real wages of workers in manufacturing industries have increased by thirty-three cents an hour.[4] But since the base period earnings of the workers in manufacturing industries were lower than that for railroad workers, the relative increase in the abilities of the two groups to purchase more goods and services has been in favor of the workers in manufacturing industries. Furthermore, taking into account the fact that the average length of the work week has risen since 1936 for workers in manufacturing industries and has fallen for workers in the railroad industry during the same period, the railroad labor organizations say that their real weekly earnings have fallen behind the rest of industry.

It is apparently even more disturbing for the railroad labor organizations to discover that from 1936 to 1952 the productivity of railroad workers (measured in terms of output per man-hour) has risen twice as much as productivity for workers in the manufacturing industries.[5]

The point has been made before that the most serious disturbances in railroad labor relations have come from the operating group, and it therefore might be in order to compare the wage changes of the nonoperating workers and the operating workers for the period 1936 to 1952.

The data reveal that from 1936 to December, 1952 the average hourly earnings of nonoperating workers increased from 59 cents to $1.87, an increase of $1.28.[6] This compares with an increase of $1.11 for the operating workers, who received 87 cents an hour in 1936 and $1.98 an hour in December, 1952. If these figures are adjusted for changes in the cost of living we find that the real wages of nonoperating workers rose by about 38 cents an hour, or about 65 percent, during this period while the real wages of the operating workers rose by 16 cents an hour, or about 18 percent. These percentage increases in real wages for the two groups can be compared with a 61 percent increase in real wages for workers in manufacturing industries. Here we find the real sore spot in the collective bargaining relationships in the railroad industry, particularly with respect to the operating workers.

At this juncture it is not necessary to discuss whether or not the railroad workers, particularly the operating group, should have received more in the form of wage increases. It is not even necessary to discuss whether these changes reflect interindustry and interoccupational shifts in manufacturing, which might have caused a rise in average hourly earnings without any changes in the basic rates. Nor is it necessary to discuss whether the narrowing of the wage gap between these groups of workers is a reflection of the delayed organization of the workers in manufacturing industries. The significant point is that the railroad workers, particularly the operating group, have observed the phenomenon and think that they have received inadequate consideration from the various arbitration and emergency boards before which they have presented their cases.

If these are the facts, how does one explain the narrowing wage differential? One answer is found in the reports of the arbitration and emergency boards who have, for a variety of reasons, failed to follow consistent, objective wage standards. Another answer is found in the fact that the railroad workers have, at least through mid-1952, been virtually deprived of their right to strike. Both of these points will be discussed in the following chapters.

CHAPTER IX

WAGE STANDARDS OF EMERGENCY BOARDS

IN THE preceding chapter it was seen that the wage position of the railroad workers, particularly the operating workers, has deteriorated in relation to wages of workers in other industries. As was indicated, this may well explain why these workers, through their unions, have fairly consistently rejected the recommendations of the emergency boards, while the carriers, in contrast, have consistently accepted the recommendations.[1] The workers, in those instances when they rejected the recommendations, have usually in the final settlements been able to obtain "a little more," but even these "bits and pieces" have been insufficient to raise the wages of the railroad workers to a level commensurate with that of the non-railroad industries.

Why have the railroads been willing to accept the emergency boards' recommendations? One reason has already been suggested in the above paragraph. A second reason is that the carriers have, under certain conditions and by application to the Interstate Commerce Commission, an opportunity to obtain rate increases if their wage costs rise significantly.

But the basic question still remains: Why have the railroad workers been unable to maintain their economic position of the 1920's and early 1930's which gave them the title "aristocrats of labor"? A basic cause—and that which will be discussed in this chapter—has been the failure of the emergency boards to establish or follow a consistent set of objective principles or standards for wage determinations. A second cause, or hypothesis, is that, *in essence*, we have had compulsory arbitration in the railroad industry until mid-1952 and this has weakened the bargaining position of labor before the emergency boards. If this second hypothesis is correct —and it will be discussed fully in the following chapter—it was even more important that the emergency boards establish certain objective standards for wage determination. For, as one writer has said, "without standards it is difficult to treat comparable cases in a comparable manner, and it is difficult to be fair to conflicting interests; or if such fairness does exist, it is not easy to convince all parties of its reality." [2]

It is true that, instead of developing a set of standards prior to the issuance of recommendations, the emergency boards have decided each case virtually on an *ad hoc* basis. An analysis of the reports of the emergency boards reveals that their final recommendations have not reflected certain consistent, objective standards. They probably are a reflection of certain "political" factors in the sense that the recommendations are influenced, directly or indirectly, either by other administrative bodies or by what the boards considered would be adequate to bring about the settlement of the disputes. It is true the the "ideal" standard would be to award to the railroad workers what they would have obtained if they had been able to bargain "freely" without the "coercive intervention" of the government, but obviously it is impossible to conform with this standard. It is recognized that the question of establishing such objective standards is a difficult one: first, there is disagreement as to appropriate standards; second, since the wage decisions affect the future operations of the industry, there may be conflicting opinions as to the impact of the decisions on, say, costs, efficiency, and prices; third, there is the question of "adding up" the results obtained from the various standards employed.[3]

In facing these problems, plus the statistical ones involved in establishing criteria for wage decisions,[4] there does not appear to be any alternative but to establish a reasonable set of objective wage standards for the settlement of railroad labor disputes. As will be pointed out below, such standards, if established, would have probably provided for greater wage increases than those actually received by the railroad workers and would have probably eliminated a great deal of labor strife.

It is reasonable to raise, at this point, two questions: First, if the railroad workers had obtained the wage increases based on certain wage criteria, would they have been satisfied? Is it not possible that they would have demanded even more? Second, would the wage increases obtained under these criteria be what they would have gotten, given "free" collective bargaining? Unfortunately, neither question can be answered directly. All that can be said with respect to the first question is that at least objective standards could be utilized as a basis for winning public support for the decisions. With respect to the second question, it might be argued that even if the wage recommended were higher than that which the union would have gotten under free collective bargaining, it may be the price that must be paid to avoid labor disputes in essential industries, and that this price might be justified in terms of potential losses, both economic as well as political, if the absence of standards yielded lower wages which in turn brought on labor conflicts.[5]

There are five principal criteria which have been considered by the emergency boards:
1. "Changes in the cost of living."
2. "Changes in the productivity of labor."
3. "The wages paid in other industries or places."
4. "The maintenance of take-home pay in the face of reduction in hours."
5. "The ability (or inability) of the employer to pay." [6]

These criteria have been employed by both the carriers and unions as well as the emergency boards themselves, with varying degrees of emphasis. The participants in the hearings have not always been consistent in urging the use of these criteria because under varying conditions any one criterion might yield different results. Similarly, emergency boards, whose decisions may reflect certain "political" considerations, have hesitated in accepting these criteria on a consistent basis for wage determination.

Each of the above-mentioned criteria will be discussed below in terms of its meaning, the statistical limitations, the extent to which positions taken by the different parties to the proceedings with respect to its use have been consistent, the attitudes of emergency boards toward these criteria, an analysis of the validity of the criteria, the economic implications of the criteria, and, finally, the extent to which the employment of, or failure to employ, these criteria resulted in any wage discrimination against the railroad worker. In general, the major national wage and rules movements in the railroad industry will be examined.

Changes in the Cost of Living

Changes in the cost-of-living index (now known as the Consumer Price Index for Moderate Income Families in Large Cities) have been, and continue to be, employed as a basis for changes in wage rates. It is to be noted that this index represents changes in the prices of a fixed basket of goods and services and does not reflect changes in the standard of living, the degree of availability of goods, or changes in the importance of particular goods in the basket.[7] The failure to understand the real meaning of the index, as well as its statistical limitations, brought on a serious controversy during World War II when the AF of L and CIO jointly attempted to "break" the Little Steel formula.[8]

It is interesting to observe the changing positions of railroad labor and the carriers on this question because they have both faced the problem of utilizing the cost-of-living criterion during periods of both rising and falling living costs.

In 1938 the railroads informed their employees that they

planned to reduce rates of pay by 15 percent. The issues eventually were presented to an emergency board, which issued its recommendations on October 29, 1938.[9] The basic point brought out by the railroads was their serious financial condition and "the one avenue that, in their judgment, remains open . . . is to effect a saving of labor costs." [10] They argued that the *real* wage of the railroad worker had increased in 1938, pointing out that in 1938 the real weekly earnings had increased on the average by more than 25 percent over 1929.[11] The employees, on the other hand, argued that "no set of index numbers can properly measure the cost of living" and does not reflect "the most important element in considering costs of living, and that is the added cost to the family of purchasing new items which have since come into customary standard of living of wage earners." [12] In other words, the unions thought that wage increases should reflect not only price changes, but also changes in the manner of living. The workers, furthermore, stressed other criteria, such as productivity increases, wage changes of other workers, the effect of a wage cut on the economy as a whole, the future outlook of the industry, and the failure of management to keep its financial house in order as a result of either past or present financial and management operations. In this case, we find that the railroads emphasized the drop in the cost of living while the labor organizations attempted to minimize the importance of it.

The 1936 emergency board, reviewing these arguments, found that the financial plight of the railroads could be solved only by measures which would go to the root of the problem and that a wage reduction did not offer any "quick financial relief." It did not employ the yardstick of productivity in deciding the case, for reasons which will be discussed below; it carefully considered and then rejected the ability-to-pay argument; it gave attention to wage rates in comparable and other industries; and it weighed the economic effects of the proposed wage cuts. On the issue of the fall in the cost of living, it accepted the unions' contention that changes in the "manner of living," as well as changes in "prices," should be considered, particularly when comparing wages over a considerable period of time.[13]

Although in this case each party to the dispute also supported its position by pointing to the general economic effect of a wage reduction—the union argued that a wage reduction in the railroad industry would set off a series of wage reductions in other industries, while the railroads argued that the lower wage costs would stimulate investment and eventually increase purchasing power—the board's report remains silent on this question.[14]

In 1941 an emergency board appointed by the President considered certain demands on the part of the railroad workers for wage increases and other changes in working conditions.[15] In this case, however, the parties switched their emphasis to cost-of-living changes, while the board was primarily concerned with the inflationary effects of a change in the wage rates and the ability of the railroad to pay a wage increase.

Again the workers brought forth a variety of criteria on which to justify a wage increase.[16] One major criterion was "the rise in the cost of living which has already ensued and the certainty of further marked increases." The carriers, however, contended that "neither at the time the wage requests were made, nor at the present time, has there been any increase in the cost of living as would support or justify a disturbance in the basic rates of pay agreed to in 1937." The carriers were willing to develop an index—a composite of price changes and revenue changes—to be used to offset future price changes. Each party used different base dates on which to estimate the change in the cost of living, apparently selecting those dates most favorable to its position.

The board, in this case, recognized certain statistical limitations of the cost-of-living index, but did not concern itself, as the 1938 board did, with the problem of changes in the manner of living. It accepted the fact that the workers experienced a rise in the cost of living and "although . . . since the outbreak of the war . . . [it] is not yet very large, there is widespread apprehension that it may be considerably extended in the year ahead." At the same time, however, the 1941 board faced up to the issue of a possible "dangerous inflation" and therefore recognized that its problem was, in the words of the board, "how to square justice to the railroad employees with the national interest." The board agreed that the changes in retail prices indicated "a need for a wage adjustment" but, noting the inflation potentialities and "the absence of a coordinated wage policy," recommended a temporary wage increase (not a change in basic wage rates) of 7½ percent for the operating workers and 9 cents per hour for nonoperating workers, which was the equivalent of about 13½ percent.[17] Although the board considered other factors, such as hazards of employment, stability of employment, comparisons with other industries, and ability to pay, a careful reading of the report reveals a considerable amount of uncertainty on the part of the board as to the adequacy and appropriateness of available data on these criteria which could be used to draw reasonable conclusions.[18]

The question arises: To what extent did the change in the cost of living play a significant role in the wage decision of this board? It seems that it was crucial. One notes that the workers pointed to a 9.7 percent increase over August, 1939, while the railroads claimed that the appropriate base was June, 1937, which would indicate an increase of 5.2 percent. The 7½ percent increase (about 8 cents per hour) for the operating workers looks like a compromise between the two figures. The 13½ percent increase for nonoperating workers apparently also reflected, to a large degree, the change in the cost of living because the board's report stresses the "understatement" of the index "for employees in the lowest wage brackets" and the greater "needs" of the low-paid group.[19]

In a subsequent report of the board, which settled the case by mediation, the board stated that in its first report it had rejected the argument of the operating workers "that the 7½ percent increase in their pay is unjust in view of the increase in the cost of living" because "if the defense program . . . is to meet with success, workers and employers alike must be prepared to make sacrifices." [20] This would seem to confirm the conclusion stated above that the criterion of the change in the cost of living was employed by the board as a basis for wage determination. It might be noted that the mediation settlement gave the operating workers an increase of 9½ cents per hour (about 1½ cents more than the Board's recommendations) and the nonoperating workers an increase of 10 cents per hour (1 cent more).[21]

In September, 1942, the nonoperating unions initiated a wage movement which eventually resulted in the establishment of an emergency board. The board considered the issues and submitted its report in mid-1943.[22] A full analysis of the issues involved was set forth in a supplemental report.[23] It is significant that the basis of the recommendations for the wage increase was *not* changes in the cost of living, but a "substantial wage inequity unfavorable" to the nonoperating railroad workers compared to "other major industries" between December, 1940, and December, 1942, as well as "unfavorable" wage differentials from 1920 to 1940.[24] The reason for the omission of any discussion of the changes in the cost of living was that at the time of the decision, wage adjustments were to be made only within the limits of the Little Steel formula which permitted cost-of-living increases of not more than 15 percent after January, 1941.[25] The wage increase of December, 1941, had apparently exhausted most of the increase allowed under the formula. The recommendation of the board was set aside by the Director of Economic Stabilization because it did not conform with the then existing stabilization policy. He then asked the board to reconsider the case; the board declined.[26]

At the time the Director of Economic Stabilization set aside the decision of the board with respect to the nonoperating unions, hearings were under way before another emergency board on the wage demands of the operating unions. This board also recognized the inequities which had accrued to the operating workers, but it decided it was bound by the determination of the Director of Economic Stabilization and recommended wage increases *within* the framework of the Little Steel formula.[27]

After the rejection of the boards' recommendations by the unions, after the appointment of a special emergency board (under the war powers of the President) which recommended larger wage increases only for workers receiving substandard wages, and after the seizure of the railroads by the President to forestall a strike, the case was eventually settled by giving the operating workers an additional 5 cents an hour and the nonoperating workers an additional 1 to 5 cents an hour "in lieu of claims for time-and-a-half pay for time over 40 hours and for expenses while away from home." [28]

What standards were utilized in the settlement of this dispute? Apparently the extra five cents awarded by the President represented nothing but the political exigencies of the time. It is clear, too, that in these cases the criterion of changes in the cost of living was firmly embedded in the recommendations of the emergency boards, reflecting the national wage policy of the period.

In 1945 two separate wage movements were initiated, one by the operating unions and another by the nonoperating organizations. In the process of negotiation and mediation the nonoperating group and three unions of the operating group accepted arbitration. The remaining two operating unions presented their case before an emergency board, whose report was issued in 1946.[29] The two arbitration boards awarded a similar increase in order to conform to this pattern.[30]

As to both the arbitration boards and the emergency board, it is quite unclear from their decisions and recommendations just what criteria were employed, though purportedly the decisions were based on changes in the cost of living, in conformance with the wage stabilization program of the so-called reconversion period. The emergency board asserted that its award of 16 cents an hour was based on changes in the cost of living, but also points out that if it considered the question of inequity and made an award of greater than 16 cents an hour its recommendation would be in conflict with the awards of the arbitration boards in the other two cases involving 85 percent of the railroad workers.[31] But if the criterion was "changes in the cost of living" how can one explain the award of 16 cents to the nonoperating workers, an increase greater than that necessary to compensate for the change in the cost of living.

In a separate opinion, two members of the arbitration board dealing with the nonoperating workers urged an increase of 30 cents an hour—11½ cents per hour to correct an inequity and 18½ cents an hour on the basis of "the clearly established prevailing measure of post-war increases." [32]

It is of interest to note that subsequent negotiations, after seizure and strike, resulted in the award of an additional 2½ cents an hour, based on the criterion, it is assumed, of the general pattern of wage increases in other industries.

Again, in 1947 three wage disputes arose. One, involving the nonoperating workers, was settled by arbitration, resulting in an award of 15½ cents per hour. This award conformed with the so-called pattern of "second round" wage increases and reflected an attempt of the arbitration board to restore to this group of railroad workers "the position they occupied in the years between 1936 and 1940 with respect to wages in other industries." [33] Later, the conductors and trainmen settled their case on the same basis.[34] However, the engineers, firemen, and switchmen presented their case to an emergency board, which, though recognizing that real wages had declined because of changes in the cost of living, awarded this group the same 15½ cents an hour because most of the railroad workers (90 percent) had already obtained this amount by arbitration or mediation.[35]

Again, the criterion of cost-of-living changes was discarded for another criterion. And again, the recommendations of the emergency board were rejected by the unions, leading to subsequent seizure and injunction and final settlement yielding an additional 15 to 20 cents per day.

In 1948 the five operating unions negotiated a settlement of a wage dispute and received an increase of 10 cents an hour, in conformance with the "third round" of wage increases.[36] The nonoperating workers went before an emergency board requesting a wage increase as well as a forty-hour work week with the maintenance of take-home pay. In its report the board noted that the evidence in justification of the wage increase was not significant. The unions based their claim on the change in the cost of living, the pattern of the "third-round" wage increases, and (with the greatest stress) the deterioration of their economic position.[37] The opinion of the board referred to the use of these criteria, as well as ability to pay and the fact that the board was awarding a forty-hour work week with the maintenance of take-home pay. On the basis of all these considerations, the board recommended a wage increase of 7 cents an hour.[38]

Although in this case the cost of living was "considered" it is certain that it played an insignificant role, though it must be recognized that the forty-hour work week issue camouflaged the wage issue.

In 1949 the conductors and trainmen initiated a movement for a wage increase and a forty-hour work week. Similar demands were made by the switchmen in a separate movement.

Emergency board hearings were held and in 1950 the board issued its recommendations.[39] In this case, too, the wage issue was beclouded by the work-week issue, but the recommendations of the board make no specific reference to the extent to which, if any, changes in the cost of living played a significant role in its determination that a forty-hour work week be established, accompanied by an increase in the basic wage rate of eighteen cents per hour.[40] Apparently, other criteria, such as the relationship of the wages of operating workers to nonoperating workers and other industrial workers, ability to pay, and productivity, were utilized, but no explanation is offered as to the importance of the several criteria.[41]

Subsequent to the report, which was rejected by the unions, the Switchmen's Union settled its case—after a strike, seizure, and injunction—receiving additional compensation and including the so-called "escalator clause," providing for quarterly adjustments of wages on the basis of changes in the cost-of-living index.[42] Also subsequent to the board's report, the firemen and engineers sought wage increases and their cases were merged by the White House with that of the conductors and trainmen in an attempt to settle the dispute. Again, after seizure and strikes—actual and so-called "sick" strikes—agreements were signed providing, among other things, for an escalator clause similar to that of the switchmen.

In late 1950 the nonoperating unions sought a wage increase, and after White House intervention the parties reached a settlement under which the workers obtained a 12½ cents an hour wage increase, plus an escalator clause similar to that described above.[43]

From the long recital above of the extent to which changes in the cost of living have been utilized as a criterion for wage determination, certain conclusions may be drawn:

1. The emergency boards either have been inconsistent, skep-

WAGE STANDARDS OF EMERGENCY BOARDS 107

tical, obscure, or have avoided the use of the criterion in their recommendations.

2. The criterion has been applied during periods when prices were actually rising or were expected to rise.
3. In the period of inflation during World War II the criterion adversely affected the wage position of the railroad workers. As was pointed out by one emergency board, "the workers in manufacturing and other non-railroad employments have shifted with relative ease to similar jobs paying higher wages," but for railroad workers "the shifts have not been as pronounced."[44] In other words, the average hourly earnings of factory workers increased more than similar rates of the railroad workers because of upgrading. Thus, from 1941 to 1945, average hourly earnings of workers in manufacturing rose by about 40 percent, while those of railroad workers increased by about 25 percent.[45]
4. Since the 1941 base-date wage for railroad workers as a group was (and today is) lower than that of factory workers, the differential spread between the two tends to grow when the criterion of maintenance of real wages is applied to all groups in the economy.

What are the economic implications of this criterion? To answer this question it is necessary to discuss first, the economic conditions of the times in which the criterion is invoked; second, the extent to which it is used; and third, the effect of such criterion on the institution of trade unionism.

In general, the criterion of changes in the cost of living has been urged by unions during periods of significant price rises and has usually been resisted by unions during periods of falling prices.[46] For this reason, the contracts in which the escalator clause is included are in most instances limited in time, and in some instances provide for a lower limit below which wages cannot fall.[47] During periods of rapidly rising prices, there has been a general consensus among economists that escalator clauses in contracts covering all industries tend to bring about an inflationary effect.[48] On the other hand, during periods of rapidly falling prices, due to a drop in demand and not to technological progress, "some economists believe that wage reductions would make the situation worse by creating expectations of further declines in prices and thus encouraging postponement of buying." [49] Other economists argue that "wage cuts, to the extent that they make possible a lower price level, make money abundant relative to the current dollar volume of production and thus help to reduce the rate of interest . . . [thereby] stimulating production." [50] Furthermore, through a reduction in labor costs, wage cuts might also cause a revival.[51] The desirability of wage cuts in a depression will not be considered further since the question is beyond the scope of this study, but it might be noted that it is highly doubtful that such a policy will ever be followed at any future time.

Since the significant question is the use of escalator clauses in periods of rising prices, and assuming that an escalator clause would tend to be inflationary, should this deter the establishment of a criterion of the maintenance of real wages in the railroad industry? It may be noted that in 1951 the escalator clause was accepted as part of a wage stabilization policy,[52] and to the extent that such policy was applicable to all industries, including the railroad industry, the railroad workers could not improve their wage position relative to other industrial workers.

As a minimum, then, it is reasonable to call for the maintenance of real earnings of the railroad workers unless the pressures of a war economy do not permit it. And under the latter condition, real wage cuts would at least be applicable to all industrial groups. Even in the absence of a general policy applicable to all labor groups and "in the absence of an overall economic discipline (including farmers and businessmen), it requires a curious kind of myopia to assume that a well organized group will single itself out to atone for the sins of the community at large." [53]

But the maintenance of real earnings of the railroad workers is not the goal of the railroad labor organizations. *Inter alia*, they seek, at a minimum, some participation in the increasing real product of the country so that they will maintain at least a constant proportion of the product. They may seek an increasing proportion of the product, even at the expense of other labor groups. To what extent have the railroad workers participated in the growing real product of the community? To what extent have the emergency boards considered this criterion?

Changes in the Productivity of Labor

There is very little disagreement among economists that there has always been, and ought to be, a fairly close relationship between the general level of productivity and the general level of wages.[54] A basic question is how *specific* increases in productivity in *particular* industries should be translated into *specific* wage increases. Or, if this should not be done, how may nationwide increases in productivity be translated into specific wage increases?

In the course of negotiations between the railroad unions and the carriers this issue has constantly arisen. And the emergency boards have also been faced with this issue. What have been the positions of the parties to the dispute with respect to productivity changes? What principles, if any, have the emergency boards followed?

The railroad unions, in each case before arbitration and emergency boards, have submitted data showing significant increases in the productivity of railroad workers and have emphasized the employment effects of the technological changes. Although the unions have urged that the productivity data should provide a basis for supporting wage increases, they have never maintained a consistent approach to the question. In fact, in one hearing the economic consultant, testifying for the labor organizations, conceded to the railroads' attorney that productivity was not an adequate basis for wage increases.[55] The carriers usually have recognized the increased productivity per man-hour, but have urged, that the mainspring of this increased productivity has been the increased investments of the railroads and that money wages have increased commensurate with productivity.[56]

A review of the decisions of the emergency and arbitration boards over the past decade and a half indicates that the members of the boards failed to develop a consistent position toward the use of the productivity criterion for determining wage increases. In part, this may have reflected the uncertain attitude of the unions and the critical attitude of the railroads, so that the net effect was either one of confusion or uncertainty in the minds of the members of the emergency boards.

In 1938 the board concluded that it was "unable to derive much aid from data relative to the growing productivity of labor" because of its inability to determine the cause for the change in productivity. It thought that to the extent that increased productivity reflected greater labor efficiency, wage increases would be justified, but to the extent it reflected greater investment, greater profits and lower prices were in order.[57]

The 1941 board, after weighing the evidence on productivity, virtually rejected the criterion when it said that "however interesting ratios of traffic units to man-hours of work may be to statisticians, such ratios offer very little help to the board in appraising the qualitative nature of the work performed by railroad men, or the quantitative magnitude of their efforts, or the specific contribution of their labor to the output of the industry." [58]

In the 1943 nonoperating workers' case, the emergency

board, in its report, made no mention of changes in productivity as a basis for a wage increase, but stressed the wage changes in other industries. However, the board, in considering the case of the operating workers, gave some attention to the criterion. But it was concerned about using it because of the difficulties of segregating these improvements (on the basis of who contributed to them) and the short-run fluctuations in productivity.[59] In recommending a wage increase, the board employed the standard of comparison with other wage groups and took into account the stabilization policy of the government.[60]

The 1946 and 1948 emergency boards, which were concerned with the operating workers, made no references to productivity and awarded wage increases on the basis of the wage patterns established in other industries, which, in turn, were based presumably on cost-of-living changes. In the 1948 nonoperating case, the emergency board, in recommending a wage increase and a forty-hour work week (with maintenance of take-home pay) makes no direct reference to productivity as a basis for its decision except for an indirect statement that it thought that the cost of implementing the forty-hour week would be eased because of the increases in productivity that would flow from the reduced work week, as well as the "resourcefulness" of management.[61]

In 1950 an emergency board, in considering the operating workers' demands for a forty-hour work week with the maintenance of take-home pay, specifically stated that "labor is entitled to participate in the results of increased output," but prefaced this conclusion with the usual remarks about statistical difficulties and the contributions of various groups to this output.[62] But just what weight was given to the productivity factor was not stated.

The settlement agreements with the nonoperating workers in 1951 and with the operating workers in 1951 and 1952 contained a clause which provided for the reopening of the wage provisions of the contracts, which were subject to a moratorium until October 1, 1953, if a national policy existed which permitted wage increases based on the so-called improvement or productivity factor. In late 1952 the railroad labor organizations sought such wage increases and in accordance with the provisions of the agreements a referee was appointed by the President of the United States to discuss the issue with the parties. The parties finally agreed that the referee would first decide whether or not a national policy did exist. If he did so find, the parties further agreed to arbitrate the issue before the same referee.

On the basis of hearings held in the early months of 1953 the referee ruled that a policy did exist and subsequently awarded the railroad workers a wage increase of four cents an hour. In essense, the referee ruled that in view of the fact that the contract period was longer than usual it was reasonable that the workers should receive some increase in real wages and share in the growing product of the country. The four cents apparently was related to the amount agreed upon in the General Motors contract. In passing, the referee stated that he was not passing any judgment on how the productivity factor should be handled in subsequent wage proceedings.[63]

The general conclusion to be drawn from this analysis of the various boards' reports is that productivity may, from time to time, have been considered in wage determinations, but the precise weight given to it is unknown. And the boards may have had good reasons for such avoidance of the standard. The statistical problems are serious.[64] How to distribute the gains in an industry—via higher wages, higher profits, or lower prices—is a difficult question to decide. Short-run relationships between wages and productivity are very uncertain.[65] Yet, the fact remains that since 1936 the railroad worker, on the average, has not participated in the increasing product of the country to the same extent as factory workers, taken as a group. From 1936 to December 1952, the real average hourly earnings of workers in manufacturing industries increased by about 61 percent, compared with an increase of 49 percent for all railroad workers.[66] The operating workers, as a group, did not fare as well since their real average hourly earnings increased by approximately 18 percent.[67] During the same period it is estimated that output per man-hour increased approximately 33 percent in manufacturing industries as contrasted with an increase of about 66 percent in the railroad industry.[68]

From these data it is quite apparent that the railroad workers, particularly the operating workers, have concluded that they have failed to participate in the increasing product of the country, despite the fact that the productivity increase in the railroad industry exceeded that of the manufacturing industries.

It should be recognized that there are inherent difficulties in tying wages to productivity, particularly in the short run, because of statistical limitations, the possible wage distortions which may develop if wages in one industry are tied to productivity in that industry, and the negative effects on output and employment.[69] In a highly competitive industry, the wage, price, and profit relationships would, in the long run, work themselves out in the market. But, in the railroad industry, where the prices are controlled by a public body and the wages of the workers are also subject to governmental determination, it would seem that the emergency boards would have to develop a formula for providing workers with a means for sharing in the increased product of the country.

There are economists who would prefer to translate productivity increases into price decreases while others suggest that a stable price level with constantly rising money and real wages is preferable.[70] But how should one handle the specific question in a specific industry? It has been suggested that "where technical advance has been more than average, money wages should rise, but not more than the average advance of productivity in the whole economy . . . ," and "where technical advance has been less than average, money wages should still rise, to give the workers their share of the general rise in productivity, but this will mean that unit costs will rise, and prices must rise accordingly." [71]

It is interesting to note that the Steel Industry Board, appointed by the President on July 15, 1949, rejected the demands of the steel workers for a wage increase and pointed out in its report that for the period under consideration "the rise in steel workers' real hourly earnings approximately matched the rise in labor productivity for the economy as a whole" and concluded "that the union failed to establish that labor's share of the steel industry's output has become inequitable." The board further pointed out that "if the productivity gains in a particular industry are higher than for the economy as a whole . . . the consumers at large should be the chief beneficiaries through lower prices for the industry's products." [72]

If this criterion had been applied in the railroad labor cases, not only would the railroad workers have improved their economic status, but the emergency boards and government would have received greater public support. Both effects would probably have been more conducive to the peaceful settlement of disputes. The absence of a specific criterion with respect to productivity, such as was employed by the Steel Board referred to above, may have played a significant role in the labor disturbances in the railroad industry for the past decade and a half.[73]

Wages Paid in Other Industries or Places

Probably the criterion most frequently considered by the emergency boards was that of "comparable wage rates." This statement would seem to contradict the facts set forth in

Chapter VIII which revealed that the economic position of the railroad workers, particularly the operating group, has deteriorated in relation to other groups of workers. But the reasons for the apparent contradiction are, first, the effect of stabilization policies on the recommendations of the emergency boards, second, the tendency of the boards to vary the emphasis given to this standard, and third, the disagreement among the boards as to the group with which to compare the railroad workers' wages.[74]

The 1938 board rejected the demands of the railroads for a 15 percent wage cut largely on the basis of comparative wage rates, and in doing so noted that there was no evidence "that railway employees have benefited more than have employees in other industries taken as a whole." [75] In this case, both the carriers and the labor organizations used the criterion in support of their positions, the unions citing post-1920 data, the carriers urging that the workers had suffered a smaller wage decrease than had other workers after the onset of the depression.[76] A considerable amount of disagreement arose between the two groups over whether to use hourly, weekly, or annual earnings, but the board ruled in favor of hourly earnings—a ruling which has been consistently followed by subsequent boards.[77]

The 1941 emergency board was careful to note the statistical and economic limitations of the use of comparative wage rates as a basis for wage determination. In fact, it rejected a list of industries selected by the 1938 board as a basis for comparison with the wages of the shop crafts. Despite these problems, it asserted that "if it appears that society has provided less well for railroad workers than for workers generally, or that the position of railroad labor has been deteriorating relatively to that of wage earners as a whole, then there is at least a presumption that railroad wages are inadequate." The board was concerned with this problem, particularly if the disadvantage had arisen within a short period of time. Nevertheless, the board tempered its wage recommendations because of its concern over the potential inflation.[78]

In the nonoperating case of 1943 the emergency board recommended a wage increase based almost exclusively on its finding that over the years the wage differential in the nonrailroad and railroad industries continued to grow.[79] This recommendation, as pointed out previously, was set aside by the Director of Economic Stabilization because the Executive Order of the President and the directives of the Director (which, incidentally, were issued while the case was pending) precluded wage changes beyond the criterion set forth in the Little Steel formula. A second emergency board, considering the case of the operating workers at the same time, also concluded that "the wages of railroad transportation workers have lagged substantially behind those of factory workers" and recognized that "the employees involved have made a strong case for a wage increase to correct gross inequities." However, in view of the directives of the Director of Economic Stabilization, the board recommended an increase in wages within the confines of the Little Steel formula.[80]

In 1946, it will be recalled, three reports were issued—two by arbitration boards covering nonoperating workers and operating workers who were members of three unions, and one by an emergency board which was concerned with the case brought before it by the other two operating unions. All three groups were awarded wage increases of 16 cents an hour. On the basis of the arbitration awards, the accompanying minority opinion in one arbitration case, and the report of the emergency board, it is apparent that each of the boards felt itself bound by the wage stabilization program in existence at that time, whereby wage changes were to be based essentially on changes in the cost of living.[81] In an opinion appended to the arbitration award for the nonoperating workers, two members asserted that the other members of the board had decided "to exclude from their consideration all evidence of inequities between railroad wage rates and wages in other industries." [82] The emergency board simply followed the pattern set by the arbitration boards because the latter boards' awards covered 85 percent of the workers and the emergency board was concerned about the creation of new inequities within the railroad industry if it failed to follow the wage pattern. In its report the emergency board commented that "there is much doubt as to what other industries may be said to be 'related' industries." [83]

Again in this case, despite the evidence of growing inequities between railroad workers and other workers, the then existing wage stabilization policies apparently prevented a higher wage award. And it is important to note that the 1946 emergency board questioned the existence of an industry whose wages could be compared with those of railroad workers, whereas previous boards were willing to select other industries for this purpose.

In 1947 the nonoperating workers settled their case by arbitration, the conductors and trainmen settled their disputes by agreement, while the other three operating unions went before an emergency board. The arbitration award to the nonoperating workers provided for an increase in wages of 15½ cents an hour "which had the effect, among others, of restoring the employees in these groups to the position they occupied in the years between 1936 and 1940 with respect to wages in other industries." [84] The conductors and trainmen subsequently accepted the same increase per hour by negotiation with the railroads directly. This 15½-cents-an-hour increase was typical of the pattern of wage increases in industry in general.[85] It is to be noted, however, that this increase did *not* restore the operating workers to their relative earnings position of the pre-1940 years. Because this pattern of 15½ cents had already been set for most of the workers in the railroad industry, the emergency board awarded the workers represented by the three operating unions a similar increase.[86] Thus, it seems that the going wage pattern, both in the railroad industry and related industries, was an important element in the recommendations of the boards.

In considering the 1948 demands of the nonoperating unions for a wage increase (in addition to a demand for a forty-hour work week with maintenance of take-home pay) the emergency board stated that "the dispute as to a wage increase must be determined primarily on the basis of the comparative increases granted in other industries in 1948, the continued rise in the cost of living since the last wage adjustment was made, and the cost to the carriers of a combined wage increase and a forty hour week." [87] The board, however, in considering the effect of the increase in basic wages due to the reduction of hours and the maintenance of take-home pay, noted that the increase would restore the nonoperating workers to the position they held, relative to that of the manufacturing industries, in 1933.[88] One notes that despite the arguments of the unions for a wage increase based on the drop in their relative earnings position since 1921, the board is concerned chiefly with what happened in other industries only within a specified time.

In 1950, in presenting demands for a forty-hour work week with maintenance of take-home pay for operating workers (chiefly yardmen), the conductors and trainmen again pointed to the "inequities" which had developed over the years, in justifying what would be an increase in basic wage rates if their request for a shorter work week were granted.[89] The unions also noted the narrowing of the differential between nonoperating workers and operating workers, which resulted chiefly from the establishment of the forty-hour work week for the former group in 1949.[90]

The board recognized the narrowing differentials and concluded that yard service workers had experienced certain inequities in relation not only to other railroad workers, but also to workers in other industries. It pointed out, however, that the narrowing of the wage gap between railroad and non-railroad workers could be explained in terms of the intensity of unionization of the 1930's among the latter group, and implied that part of the narrowing is reasonable and justifiable. As a result, instead of recommending an increase of approximately 31 cents per hour which would permit maintenance of take-home pay under a forty-hour week and which, according to the union, would "not suffice to close the gap of increase in real wages, although it will minimize the inequity that obtains," the board granted a wage increase of 18 cents an hour.[91]

It is apparent from an analysis of the emergency boards' reports that the railroad workers and the carriers have been subjected to the criterion of "comparative wage" rates by the emergency boards during the past ten or fifteen years. But whenever the criterion was accepted, particularly in terms of developing differentials, other factors, particularly the stabilization programs of the government, prevented wage increases based on the criterion. On the other hand, when the governmental influence was removed, there was a tendency for the boards to consider only the patterns of wage increases then current, and in one instance this criterion was agreed to voluntarily by two operating unions. Finally, as in the 1950 case, when neither governmental wage policies existed nor going wage patterns were dominant, a new element is introduced, namely, whether or not the narrowing of wage differentials over the years is justifiable and correct from an economic point of view. It would seem that the latter criterion is the most correct since there are significant limitations to attempting the maintenance of wage differentials among industries over a period of time.[92] But it must be apparent that shifting interpretations and uses of a standard are not conducive to labor's acceptance of wage recommendations by the emergency boards.

The Maintenance of Take-Home Pay in the Face of a Reduction in Hours

The issue of whether or not the take-home pay of yard workers should be maintained with a reduction in the work week from forty-eight to forty hours took over two years to resolve, after an emergency board issued its recommendations.[93] On this issue we find a basic disagreement not only between the parties to the dispute but also between two emergency boards, whose recommendations were made within a period of eighteen months.

The labor organizations have argued that the maintenance of take-home pay in the face of a reduction in hours was a policy followed under the NRA and was a common practice in other industries.[94] The carriers, however, submitted data designed to disprove this contention.

In December, 1948, in a case involving nonoperating workers, an emergency board recommended a reduction in the work week with the maintenance of take-home pay.[95] The basis for the decision, affecting about one million workers, was, first, that the forty-hour work week "is the prevailing practice in American industry"; second, "it is an established working condition in many transportation industries"; third, there has been a continuous decline in employment in this group; and, finally, the maintenance of take-home pay with such reduction in hours "has generally been the practice in other industries." [96]

On the other hand, the 1950 board, considering a similar request for the operating yard workers, also recognized that the forty-hour work week was an "established pattern in American industry," and, more particularly, already existed for more than two thirds of the workers in the railroad industry.[97] With respect to the maintenance of take-home pay, the board apparently rejected the conclusion of the 1948 board that it had been a widespread practice. It explained its rejection of the demand for the maintenance of take-home pay and its failure to accept the recommendation of the 1948 board on the ground that the evidence before the board and the occupational group involved were different. It considered other factors such as technological displacement, stability of employment, comparative wages, and costs of the carrying out of the recommendations.[98]

With respect to the criterion of maintaining take-home pay in the face of a reduction in hours, the economic effects must be carefully considered. The economic effects, in terms of production and employment, via the cost function, depend on a variety of factors, e.g., the elasticity of demand for labor.[99] But despite such possible effects, the evidence is clear that one group of railroad workers found that the criterion applied to another group was not fully applicable to it. And regardless of the merits of the distinction, such apparent inconsistency does not provide a basis for stable labor relations and is not conducive to the acceptance by labor of the recommendations of the emergency boards.

Ability to Pay

The criterion of "ability to pay" has been considered in every railroad wage case presented to emergency and arbitration boards. And these boards have been faced with serious questions: How much significance should be attached to the criterion? Should ability to pay be considered from the short-run or long-run point of view? Should the question be considered in terms of past or future profits? Should individual railroads be considered? How can one determine what the profits will be in the future, given the variables involved? What standard of profitability should be employed?

These questions, though difficult and complex in general, are exceedingly thorny in the railroad industry. The industry's general rate level is subject to control by the Interstate Commerce Commission, while its actual rates are influenced by competitive conditions.[100] Further, the industry is beset with a large amount of fixed capital, "irrevocably sunk in the enterprise," and just how much return should be allowed such capital is difficult to determine.[101]

Despite these questions and difficulties, the emergency boards have always given consideration to the question of ability to pay, although the degree of attention given to the principle has varied from board to board. The carriers have consistently asserted that they could not afford to grant wage increases and have generally pointed to the fact that the railroad earnings (based on return on investment) have been lower than those of other industries for a variety of reasons and have urged the necessity for adequate earnings in order to effectuate the policies set forth in the Transportation Act of 1940.[102] The labor organizations, on the other hand, have also pointed to the same law which calls for, *inter alia*, the encouragement of "fair wages and equitable working conditions." [103] The employees' position has, however, shifted in emphasis from time to time. For example, in the 1938 case, faced with the possibility of a wage reduction, the labor organizations argued that the financial straits in which the railroads found themselves resulted from unwise financial practices in the past and basic inefficiencies in management.[104] The unions have, at times, indicated willingness to assist the railroads in an attempt to secure rate increases.[105] On the other hand, in 1941 and 1943, for example, the employees pointed to the improved financial position of the railroads, and used this as a basis for demanding an increase in wages.[106] In general, though, it may be said that the employees have been extremely reluctant to accept as a criterion the ability of the railroads to pay desired wage increases. They have urged, instead, that the wage increases could be paid out of current earnings, and if the earnings are inadequate, the railroads' general rate level should be raised.

Similarly, there have been, if not inconsistencies on the part of the emergency boards, at least varying degrees of emphasis on the role that the criterion of ability to pay should play in wage determination. In the 1938 case, the board considered both the long-run and short-run financial condition of the railroads and indicated that temporary financial difficulties must be absorbed by the industry and not by the workers. Furthermore, it took note of the fact that since the case was initiated, there appeared to be a revival in railroad traffic. The board concluded that if the financial difficulties continued, the possibilities of wage reductions "would have to be explored." [107]

In 1941, however, the board was skeptical of both the short-run and long-run earnings potentialities of the railroads and therefore recommended *temporary* wage increases for fear that, if the wage rates were increased permanently, there would be little possibility, if any, of decreasing them later in the face of decreased earnings.[108] On the other hand, the 1943 board, in considering the wage demands of the nonoperating workers, stated that "the financial condition of the railroads has a bearing on wage policy, but it is not a critical and determining factor." [109] It agreed with the employees' position "that the maintenance of unduly depressed wage levels would be an unjustifiable method of extending financial aid to the railroad." Further, the 1943 board agreed that the criterion was not of primary importance, but indicated that it thought that wage increases should flow from increased revenues and that downward wage revisions might be in order when revenues fell.[110]

In 1946, when the emergency board recommended a wage increase of 16 cents an hour to conform with the pattern set by the arbitration boards (which based their decision, in large part, on changes in cost of living in conformance with the stabilization program), no mention was made of the railroads' ability to pay, although the carriers pointed out that they would have to seek relief, in the form of rate increases, if the 16-cents-an-hour award was made.[111]

In 1948 an emergency board recommended a wage increase to the operating workers equal to that awarded by an arbitration board and agreed upon between two labor organizations and the railroads, without reference to ability to pay. But later in 1948, in considering the demand of the nonoperating workers for a wage increase, along with the forty-hour work week demand, another emergency board carefully considered the question of costs involved and awarded the forty-hour work week, with the maintenance of take-home pay, on the basis of an optimistic view of future productivity, "resourcefulness of management," and the general financial position of the railroads. In considering the wage issue separately, the board recommended a wage increase. The amount was lower than the pattern of third-round increases because the board took account of the costs involved in changing to a forty-hour work week.[112]

Finally, in 1950, an emergency board, considering a request for a forty-hour work week, rejected the demands of the operating workers, to a large extent upon the basis of ability to pay. The board explained that the ability of the railroads to offset the increased costs resulting from the reduced work week in the form of compressing, deferring, or postponing work for operating workers was considerably less than for nonoperating workers. The board was far more impressed with the low rate of return of the railroads than was the 1948 board, and was less optimistic about the role that future increases in productivity would play in the reduction of costs.[113]

With respect to the criterion of ability to pay in wage determinations, we find it used in some instances, neglected in others. It is given considerable weight in one case, lesser weight in another. The role that future earnings, as well as the significance of current earnings, has played in the boards' recommendations varied considerably.

In virtually all the cases the financial data submitted by the railroads have been based on reports of the Interstate Commerce Commission and have provided the basis for the board's analysis of the railroads' ability to pay. There was, however, one exception—the 1943 nonoperating case—in which the board raised such questions as the propriety of deducting taxes before arriving at a net income figure, the failure to deduct depreciation in calculating rate of return on investment, the inclusion in book value of certain nonexistent values, and the correctness of calculating the average rate of dividend return on the basis of stated book value.[114]

OTHER CRITERIA

In the course of emergency board proceedings other criteria have, from time to time, been suggested, particularly by the labor organizations, as a basis for wage increases: the substandard annual earnings of some workers, supported by budget studies; the irregularity of employment of some groups of workers; and the hazards of employment. Both parties to the disputes have consistently disagreed with the significance and interpretation of the data submitted and the emergency boards have generally disregarded these criteria in their wage recommendations.

CONCLUSION

The preceding analysis reveals the failure of the emergency and arbitration boards to follow consistently certain objective criteria in their wage determinations. The statistical limitations call for judicious handling of the data. Short-run and long-run relationships must also be carefully considered. The economic effects of the use of the criteria are at times vague and uncertain, depending upon either unknown or unpredictable variables. The need to consider carefully the wage-price-profit relationships is clear. Yet, despite all of these limitations in the development and use of criteria in wage determinations, there does not appear to be any attempt to develop standards. And this failure may well have played a part in the deterioration in the economic position of the railroad workers and the increasing dissatisfaction of the railroad workers with the wage recommendations of the emergency boards.

The need for developing such criteria is great when the wages of workers are influenced by the coercion of government. For when wages are determined freely between labor and management, the criterion is quite simple: the economic cost to either side for failing to come to an agreement.[115] But if the wages are determined as a result of governmental "coercive intervention" objective criteria must be established. It would be desirable to have them worked out "primarily by labor and management if the principles of collective bargaining are to be preserved." [116]

CHAPTER X

COMPULSION IN THE SETTLEMENT OF RAILWAY LABOR DISPUTES

TESTIFYING in 1950 before a Senate committee on a bill designed to prohibit strikes and to provide for the compulsory arbitration of labor disputes in the railroad industry, a spokesman for the railroads stated that "certainly for the past ten years, at least, you have actually had what amounts to compulsory arbitration in the railroad industry." [1] This statement is in contrast with the view of the National Mediation Board that "nowhere in these procedures [under the Railway Labor Act] is there any compulsion on either party to settle the dispute. On the contrary, the law is based upon the principle of free and untrammeled collective bargaining. There is nothing in the law which abridges the right of employees to strike." [2] There apparently is a gap between the law and the reality of free collective bargaining in the industry. It is the purpose of this chapter to describe how this gap was bridged by the development of compulsion by law, as well as compulsion by the executive office of the President.

A study of the major wage movements of the past decade reveals that, with few exceptions, the cases were decided by the intervention of the President, after the recommendations of emergency boards had been issued. Such intervention took place, at times, after a strike was in process. In some instances, no strike actually took place, but was threatened. In other cases, regardless of whether or not a strike took place, government seizure forced a settlement of the disputes. And in some cases, it was necessary to obtain a court injunction in order to get the workers back on their jobs. There was even one case in which the injunction was violated and successful contempt proceedings initiated.

Thus, a pattern emerges. If the recommendations of the emergency board are rejected, the railroad unions, after the required thirty days' delay, may call a strike. If the strike takes place, or if the government thinks the strike may take place, government seizure may follow. After seizure, the government, if still faced with a strike or threatened strike, may petition the court for an injunction. Upon issuance of the injunction, any further strike activity on the part of the union may be subject to contempt proceedings and possible fine, if found guilty.

How had this compulsion and the virtual elimination of the right to strike in the railroad industry developed? What effect have these conditions had upon collective bargaining relationships in the railroad industry? Are there defects in the present Railway Labor Act which have brought about a situation where genuine collective bargaining has been virtually destroyed? What proposals have been made to meet the problem of strikes in industries affecting the public interest? How adequate are these proposals? Why has Congress been reluctant to enact a compulsory arbitration law, in any industry? These questions will be considered in this and the following chapters.

THE LEGAL DOCTRINE

The legal right of the President to seize the railroads—at least until mid-1952—has been justified on two grounds: first, under the Act of August 29, 1916, the President may, in time of war, take possession and assume control and operation of any system of transportation;[3] second, it is alleged that the President of the United States, under the constitution, may, in circumstances of grave emergency, take whatever action is necessary to protect "the life of the community." [4]

The seizures of the past decade have been justified primarily by the Act of August 29, 1916, which provided for the seizure of railroads during wartime. This statutory power was eliminated by Congress in 1952. But prior to this repeal, until peace treaties had been formally signed with Germany and Japan, the United States was technically still at war.[5] Furthermore, any injunction issued by the courts to enjoin the workers was considered valid and not subject to the provisions of the Norris–La Guardia Act because, after seizure, the railroad workers were technically employed by the government.[6] Under such conditions, the Supreme Court has held that the Norris–La Guardia Act is not applicable. (See *United States v. United Mine Workers*, 330 U.S. 258, 1947.)

On May 10, 1948, the District Court of the United States (District of Columbia) issued a temporary injunction restraining three operating unions from striking on railroads already seized by the government. Subsequently, the question of a permanent injunction was argued before the Court and on July 2, 1948, the Court issued such an injunction based essentially on the United Mine Workers case.[7]

There appears little doubt that, when the United States was technically still at war and the President did have the statutory power to seize the railroads, an injunction could be secured to prevent any concerted strike activity. Further, any violation of the injunction was subject to contempt proceedings. However, one question still open for discussion is the right of the President to seize the railroads and/or obtain an injunction against the employees in time of peace.

This question revolves around the issue of whether or not the President has "inherent power" under the Constitution to seize and/or to enjoin a strike "in circumstances of grave emergency to take necessary action to protect the life of the community." [8] In the 1948 seizure of the railroads, such a position was taken by the federal government, although it also justified the seizure and demand for an injunction under the war powers of the President. And, as indicated above, the District Court sustained this position.[9]

The government's position—at least until June 1952—had been supported by the statements of two Attorney Generals of the United States, as well as by the opinion of the District Court in the railroad case. In 1939 Attorney General Murphy, in response to a request of the Senate for a statement of "what executive powers are made available to the President under his proclamation of national emergency," stated that

the Executive has . . . powers derived not from statutory grants, but from the Constitution. It is universally understood that the constitutional duties of the Executive carry with them the constitutional powers necessary for their proper performance. These constitutional powers have never been specifically defined, and in fact, cannot be since their extent and limitations are largely dependent upon conditions and circumstances. In a measure this is true with respect to most of the powers of the Executive, both constitutional and statutory. The right to take specific action might be the absolute duty of the Executive to take such action.[10]

In 1949, upon the request of the Senate Committee of Education and Labor, Attorney General Clark submitted a report and opinion on S. 249, designed to repeal the Taft-Hartley Law.[11] Citing both the statement of Attorney General Murphy and the decision in the United Mine Workers case, Clark said that "the inherent power of the President to deal with emergencies that might affect the health, safety, and welfare of the entire nation is exceedingly great." He stated further, that "in a national crisis, the United States would have access to the courts to protect the national health, safety, and welfare. I say this because it is my belief that access to its own court is always available to the United States, in the absence of a specific statutory bar depriving the government of the right to seek the aid of the Federal Courts in such critical situations." Although there is a difference of opinion with respect to this "inherent power" of the President, the opinion of the District Court in the railroad case in 1948 sustained this view.

The District Court pointed out that workers "can strike under the Norris–La Guardia Act, even when it would cause great inconvenience, and a great loss of production and distribution, but they can't go to a point, in order to have their way, however much right they have on their side, they can't go to the point of adopting a process which would disintegrate society itself, and that is the situation here." [12] This statement tended to support the position that an essential industry cannot be closed down by strike, even with the protection of the Norris–La Guardia Act.

Furthermore, there are some *dicta* in the case which, in effect, state that the railroad workers, having had their day in court (via the procedures of the Railway Labor Act), should not be permitted to strike. The Court was careful to point out that "in face of the fact that the unions have had the benefit" of the consideration of their case by several impartial bodies "they sent out that notice" to stop work.[13] In a strike situation involving only one union and one railroad, a United States District Court issued a preliminary injunction in 1950 against the Switchmen's Union on similar grounds.[14]

It is true that in the famous steel seizure case the Supreme Court rejected the government's claim that it had the right to seize the various steel companies.[15] The decision of the Court pointed out that there was no statutory authority to seize, and regardless of the emergency, the President could not, in the absence of specific authority, take over the steel industry. This would seem to reject the "inherent power" argument. But it should be noted that in the various concurring opinions there were references to the facts that under the Taft-Hartley Law no authority to seize was granted in the so-called national emergency section of the law and that the government had certain seizure powers under the Selective Service Act.

In recognizing the general principle that the Supreme Court only passes judgment on the facts in a specific case, it does not necessarily follow that the rejection of the "inherent power" argument in the steel case would automatically result in the rejection of the same argument if, and when, the railroads were once again seized. However, the elimination by Congress of the power that the President had to seize railroads under the 1916 statute after the steel decision would seem to indicate the Congressional viewpoint.

During the early part of 1953 several strikes on individual railroads had broken out and in no instance was there any talk of seizure. It is apparent that there were no serious "emergencies," if one were to use the newspaper coverage of the strikes as a yardstick. On October 1, 1953, the present contracts between the railroads and their employees expired and another national wage and rules movement has already gotten under way. What the results will be, in terms of collective bargaining relationships, is uncertain. And whether a nationwide railroad strike, if it did threaten or did occur, would bring into the picture the issue of "seizure" is a question which cannot be answered now. It will, however, be interesting to observe whether the attitudes of the parties toward collective bargaining change in view of the Supreme Court's decision on seizure.

It is clear that up to mid-1952 the railroad unions had lost the one "weapon" of collective bargaining which unions have in enforcing their demands, namely, the right to strike. During the past decade, the unions faced the alternative of accepting the recommendations of the emergency boards appointed by the President or of rejecting them in the hope of getting more from the intervention of the President—which last they have done at times in the past. But later the Presi-

COMPULSION IN SETTLEMENT OF DISPUTES 133

dential determination became the decision and the union's resistance to this determination proved of little avail since the President had the power to seize the railroads and to obtain an injunction against the unions, thereby preventing a strike.

The Intervention of the President

The intervention of the office of the President in labor disputes is not novel and history is replete with such cases in the railroad and other industries.[16] During the past decade, the intervention of the President in railway labor disputes has been extensive.

What are the effects of such intervention? According to Slichter there are three.[17] In the first place, the President does not have the opportunity to study the facts and give careful consideration to the issues involved. Second, the President is not generally the person "whom the two sides would select as a neutral," chiefly because "his prestige is so great that a decision by him is virtually an order." In the 1943 case, for example, three of the unions refused to accept the President as an arbitrator. The role of a President as an arbitrator, in the opinion of one writer, is "compulsory arbitration in its most undesirable form, namely, by a political officer of the government." Finally, the possibility of Presidential intervention might be an impetus for either of the parties to the dispute to refuse to settle the case at any lower level.

The extent to which the political office of the President may be employed in the settlement of railway labor disputes, and the repercussions flowing from such intervention are illustrated in the 1946 and 1949–1950 cases involving the operating workers. According to one version of the 1946 case, the President of the Brotherhood of Railroad Trainmen refused to arbitrate (as did the other three operating unions) and expressed an intention to push the case to the point of a strike and then to force the President to settle the strike on some relatively satisfactory basis, as Franklin D. Roosevelt had done in a similar situation in December, 1943.[18] The case did reach the President's office and a stenographic transcript of the conversation between the President of the United States and the union officials reveals the following commitments by the President: If the unions postponed a scheduled strike he, the President, would get more for the unions than the last offer; if the strike were postponed and then renewed, the President would protect the unions from any possible prosecution under the Smith-Connally Act.[19] Despite the postponement of the strike on these assurances, no settlement was forthcoming and the unions renewed their strike threat. Whereupon the President asked Congress for legislation to draft the railroad workers. The strike collapsed and the workers settled on the President's terms.[20]

Similarly, in 1949–1950, after the emergency board's recommendations on the forty-hour work week and the wage issue were rejected by the conductors and the trainmen, the case went to the White House for settlement. After negotiations proved fruitless, and after the unions threatened a strike, the railroads were seized. Finally, a settlement was reached, but this settlement was rejected by the unions' general chairmen. One reason alleged for the rejection was the inclusion of a clause in the agreement which would make Dr. John R. Steelman, a Presidential assistant, the arbitrator of any future rules disputes.[21] After the agreement was signed by the union officials, one official was reported to have said that "when you're under government control you take what the government gives you." [22] Subsequently, at a hearing before a Senate committee investigating the two-year dispute, another union official asserted, "I never thought I would be blackjacked in the east wing of the White House, but that has been my unfortunate experience in the handling of these negotiations." He also stated that Dr. Steelman implied "that the President of the United States would ram the settlement down our throat." [23] The fear was expressed by another union official, testifying before the same committee, that the White House was making the Railway Labor Act a compulsory law because President Truman, according to the witness, felt that the recommendations of the emergency boards should be binding.[24]

These two cases illustrate the difficulties which are encountered when labor disputes go to the office of the President for settlement. The results, even if settlements are achieved, are not conducive to stable collective bargaining, particularly if one or both parties think that they were forced to accept the settlement. And in those instances when Presidential intervention has failed, the labor dispute continues and seemingly no place remains for the final resolution of the dispute. Apparently, the Senate committee referred to above attempted to settle the 1950 dispute informally. Such a method of settling the dispute is completely outside the procedures of the Railway Labor Act.[25]

Thus, we find that until mid-1952 the courts had virtually prohibited strikes in the railroad industry. In addition, the White House had taken a position that the unions should accept the recommendations of the emergency boards, or at a minimum accept the settlement proffered by the President. Finally, with the statutory power available to him, the President could either seize the railroads and/or seek injunctive relief from the courts. The conclusion is not unwarranted that we had, for all intents and purposes, compulsory arbitration in the railroad industry.

Although it would seem that the railroad labor organizations today have regained the right to strike (the issue of government seizure of railroads, however, is yet to be resolved conclusively), there is still considerable pressure upon the unions to accept the recommendations of the emergency boards. And if the prestige of the office of the President of the

United States is to be utilized to bring about such acceptance (and it seems to be the objective of the National Mediation Board to achieve this), it would seem essential that emergency boards, in their recommendations, make every effort to offer to the unions the equivalent of what the unions would be able to obtain if they were free of any "coercive intervention" by the government. The establishment of criteria agreed upon by the two parties (as suggested in the previous chapter), would be one way by which the problem could be approached.

It is apparent from the recital of some of the events of the past decade that there has been little, if any, genuine collective bargaining in the railroad industry. It has been suggested, so far, that the deterioration of the earnings position of the railroad workers, the lack of consistent, objective standards for wage determination by emergency fact-finding boards, and the intervention of the courts and the President have contributed to the breakdown in collective bargaining.

CHAPTER XI

BREAKDOWN OF GRIEVANCE PROCEDURES [1]

COLLECTIVE BARGAINING has two aspects: it is a method by which wages are set and it is a method by which certain rules and practices are established in order to prevent management from acting arbitrarily and to insure the security of the workers and the union organizations.[2] In the railroad industry, as in other industries, there has developed a comprehensive system of what has been called "industrial jurisprudence," [3] which has been described in Chapter IV. An elaborate system of working rules naturally requires a procedure for the settlement of grievances arising out of the interpretation and application of the rules. Over the years there has evolved a system of adjustment boards designed for this purpose, and the Railway Labor Act, as amended, has specifically provided for the establishment of such boards.[4]

It is generally agreed that the procedure for the settlement of grievances differs from the negotiations for a collective bargaining agreement "primarily in its approach." [5] The grievance procedure is intended to solve problems within the framework of principles of the collective bargaining agreement, on an equitable basis and not on the basis of the economic strength of either of the parties to the dispute.[6] An examination of grievance procedures in various industries has revealed that certain principles have evolved in the settlement of disputes arising out of the interpretation and application of the terms of collective bargaining agreements.[7] First, it is essential that all of the participants involved accept and have a complete understanding of the procedures. Second, both parties to the dispute should agree not to resort to "unilateral coercion" in order to obtain their ends. Third, the successful performance of any grievance procedure requires that grievances be handled promptly. Fourth, it is desirable that the number of grievances be limited so as not to overload the system. Finally, there should be fair consideration of the issues so that decisions are acceptable to both sides. These principles represent an ideal against which one might compare the performance of the adjustment boards in the railroad industry. It is the purpose of this chapter to evaluate this performance.

After a description of the procedures established for the settlement of grievances in the railroad industry, an evaluation of the procedures will be made. The analysis indicates, first, that the principles described above have not been followed in the settlement of grievances in the railroad industry; second, that this failure to conform to these principles reflects a basic conflict between the parties over the working rules; and third, that the various proposals offered for the improvement of the procedures would not solve the problem because they fail to take into consideration the causes of the breakdown in the grievance procedures.

Provisions of the Railway Labor Act, as Amended, for the Settlement of Grievances

The Railway Labor Act, as amended in 1934, completely revised the procedures to be followed in the resolution of grievance disputes arising out of the interpretation and application of collective bargaining agreements entered into between the railroad labor organizations and the carriers. A National Railroad Adjustment Board was established on a permanent basis and consisted of thirty-six members. Half were to be selected by the labor organizations and the other half by the carriers. Each member of the board was to be compensated by the party he represented. The board was composed of four divisions, each of which had jurisdiction over disputes involving different groups of workers. The First Division had jurisdiction over disputes "involving train- and yard-service employees of the carriers; that is, engineers, firemen, hostlers, and outside hostler helpers, conductors, trainmen, and yard-service employees." The employees in this group are generally referred to as the "operating workers." The Second and Third Divisions had jurisdiction over disputes involving the so-called "non-operating workers." The former division was concerned chiefly with disputes involving workers employed in the shops, the latter division with "station, tower, and telegraph employees, train dispatchers, maintenance-of-way men, clerical employees, freight handlers, express, station and store employees, signalmen, sleeping car conductors, sleeping car porters, and maids and dining car employees." The Fourth Division was concerned with disputes involving workers employed by the carriers engaged in transportation by water and all other workers who were not under the jurisdiction of the other divisions.

The establishment of a permanent, national board in 1934 rather than voluntary, local, or system boards was a significant change. The 1926 law provided for the establishment of adjustment boards only upon agreement between the parties. As a result very few such boards were set up, primarily because of the aversion of the unions to local or system boards.[8] A second significant change was the provision for the selection of a "referee" if, and when, a board was deadlocked. Experience under the 1926 law had shown that bipartisan boards were frequently deadlocked with the result that certain decisions were never forthcoming.[9]

The 1934 amendments did not provide for the compulsory arbitration of grievance disputes. The revised law stated that such disputes "shall be handled in the usual manner up to and including the chief operating officer of the carrier." If, however, an adjustment is not reached, "the disputes may be referred . . . to the appropriate divisions of the Adjustment

Board." This method for the adjustment of grievance disputes is not compulsory arbitration (voluntary or involuntary) nor is it completely free of compulsion. Since *either* party may submit a case to the adjustment board, the other party is compelled to appear before the board and submit to its determinations.

Finally, the amendments provided that "if a carrier does not comply with an order of the Adjustment Board . . . the petitioner . . . may file in the District Court of the United States . . . a petition" for the enforcement of the award.

The Railway Labor Act directs the Adjustment Board to establish its own rules of procedure and, accordingly, such rules were issued in 1934.[10] The rules are simple and informal. If a grievance dispute has not been settled "on the property" it is referred to the Board, either in a "joint statement" of facts or as an "ex parte submission." Under the former type of submission both parties present the facts, and if there is disagreement, each party makes his own submission. When an ex parte submission is made—and this is the typical type of submission—the party states the facts to the Board and notifies the other party that such submission has been made. The other party does not obtain a copy of the petitioner's statement of facts but may answer within a specified period of time. Oral hearings are held if either party or both of the parties request them. Hearings are then held before the appropriate board and if the board is deadlocked the case is then referred to a referee, who is usually hired on an *ad hoc* basis.[11]

Evaluation of the Grievance Procedures

ACCEPTANCE AND UNDERSTANDING

As noted above, an important principle in the settlement of grievance disputes is the acceptance and understanding of the procedures by the parties to the disputes. Such acceptance and understanding does not exist with respect to the grievance procedures in the railroad industry. In the first place, the 1934 amendments, particularly those concerned with the settlement of grievances, did not have the full support of management. It has been said that "the representatives of the railway labor organizations approved of the scheme [for the revision of the adjustment procedures] in its more essential features, but the representatives of the carriers for the most part expressed the opinion that such a board might do more harm than good." [12]

Second, there is a basic disagreement between the carriers and the railroad labor organizations as to the proper function of the Adjustment Board. The representatives of the railroad labor organizations have stated that "it is our very definite conclusion . . . that the Adjustment Board never was intended to function as a court of equity but rather that it should operate as a continuation of the conference room method employed upon the various properties where men and management 'talk things through,' argue the meaning of rules, discuss the application in effect under the rules, and finally attempt to reach an 'equitable' adjustment based upon our practical knowledge of how things are done 'back home.'" [13] The union representatives argue that this was the intention of Congress and refer to the fact that the Adjustment Board was to consist of representatives of labor and management (and not public officials), that the Act does not give the Board the right to issue subpoenas or administer oaths, and that the Act does not spell out any procedures to be followed by the Board. The carriers, however, take an opposite view. They assert that "it is the duty of this Board to hear and decide disputes . . . in strict conformity with the agreements between the particular carrier and employees involved applicable to the issues in question, giving due consideration to the practices and precedents established on that property in the administration of the applicable rule or rules of the agreement under which the dispute originated." [14]

In other words, the carriers do not think that "horse-trading" and "negotiation" of the disputes are in order. They charge that the labor representatives have used the Board not to interpret the rules but to extend them.[15] The labor organizations are opposed to a strict interpretation of the agreements because, for one thing, they are seeking a uniform application of the rules to all of the railroads, and for another, they fear that any variation in the application of the rules will be used as an entering wedge by the carriers to relax or eliminate the rules.

Third, because of the backlog of cases and the delays in decisions, or possibly in those instances where the labor organizations are uncertain of the merits in the disputes, the labor organizations have, at times, avoided the machinery of the Adjustment Board and sought the settlement of grievances through other machinery. Since the law does not require them to use the Adjustment Board, the railroad labor organizations at times have accumulated grievances, placed them on a strike ballot, and worked through the emergency board procedures of the Railway Labor Act.[16] For example, during the fiscal year 1949–1950, six of the eleven emergency boards created by the President were concerned with grievances rather than changes in collective bargaining agreements. In most instances, the boards have refused to consider these cases and have suggested that they be referred to the Adjustment Board. But in some cases they have proceeded either to mediate the disputes or to issue recommendations for the settlement of them.[17] The emergency boards have consistently warned of the tendency on the part of the unions to bring grievances before them, to strike or to threaten a strike in such cases, and have indicated that a continuation of this procedure for the settlement of grievance disputes might bring about "a complete nullification of the Railway Labor Act." [18] This avoidance of the grievance procedures is illustrated in one case presented to an emergency board in which the strike ballot involved 1,400 grievances which had not been settled "on the properties." [19]

Finally, it is alleged by the unions that in many instances railroad management refuses to accept the awards of the Adjustment Boards.[20] The position of the railroads is that in view of the fact that many awards may result in a heavy financial burden on the railroads, they should have an opportunity to have them reviewed by the courts.[21] As mentioned previously, the issue usually comes before the courts when the railroad labor organizations seek the enforcement of the award. But the unions, in an attempt to avoid court review of the Adjustment Board's awards and to prevent delay in the carrying out of the award, frequently use their economic strength, via a strike or threatened strike, to obtain their ends.

The original lack of agreement between the parties with respect to the 1934 amendments, the disagreement as to the proper function of the Adjustment Board, the avoidance of the procedures established under the law, and the problem of the enforcement of the awards, indicate a considerable lack of understanding and acceptance of the grievance procedures in the railroad industry.

AVOIDANCE OF UNILATERAL COERCION

Any successful grievance procedure requires that the parties to the dispute avoid the use of unilateral coercion in order to obtain acceptance of their demands. This principle has been violated many times. A major complaint of the railroads has been that the railroad labor organizations have threatened to strike, or actually have gone on strike, either before or after the procedures have been invoked.[22] The National Mediation Board has pointed out that "some of the [labor] organizations have withdrawn cases pending before the [Adjustment Board] and declined to submit new cases, preferring to secure settlements by direct handling with the carrier management. Where such negotiations fail, strikes are sometimes threatened." [23]

At this point it is not necessary to go into the merits of the issue, but merely to point out that when one side uses the threat of a strike to win a grievance dispute, a basic principle of grievance procedure is violated, and to indicate that under the present grievance procedures strikes have either been threatened or have taken place.

PROMPTNESS IN SETTLEMENT OF GRIEVANCES

A third standard to be met in any successful procedure for the settlement of grievances is promptness. For reasons which will be discussed below, there has accumulated a large backlog of cases, primarily in the First Division, which is concerned with disputes involving the operating workers. The problem is most acute in this division because the rules which it must interpret are more complex and more highly developed. On June 30, 1952, a total of 4,717 cases was pending before the Board, of which 4,186 involved workers on the roads and in the yards (Division 1).[24] At the rate at which such cases have been disposed of by the First Division in the fiscal year 1952, it would take the Board more than two years to handle the backlog, aside from the number of new cases arising.[25] And during the past eighteen years of the operation of the Adjustment Board new cases have been docketed at an average of more than 2,000 each year.[26] The National Mediation Board states that "the backlog continues large. . . . A large backlog means long delays in considering cases and issuing awards. These delays often run into years. Employees and their representatives, tiring of such long delays, have resorted to other techniques to secure settlements." [27]

LIMITING THE NUMBER OF CASES

It is desirable, as noted earlier, that grievances be settled on the property and that a limited number of cases be referred to a board for settlement. Failure to conform to this standard results in an overloading of the grievance machinery, accom-

BREAKDOWN OF GRIEVANCE PROCEDURES 145

panied by an accumulation of a backlog of cases. Over the eighteen-year period, from 1935 to 1952, 38,360 cases were docketed with the Adjustment Board, of which 33,653 were disposed of in one way or another.[28] Since 1946 there has been a steady increase in the number of cases docketed, rising from 1,011 cases in that year to 2,815 cases in 1952. At the end of the fiscal year 1952, the number of cases pending before the board (4,717) was the highest since 1945. These data would seem to indicate that the Board, as presently constituted, is not capable of handling the task for which it is responsible.

FAIR CONSIDERATION OF ISSUES

Finally, any grievance procedure must provide for the fair consideration of the issues so that the awards are acceptable to both parties. But the disagreement as to the proper function of the Board, as discussed above, does not provide the basis for a fair consideration of each case. In addition, the bipartisan make-up of the Adjustment Board and the fact that the members of the Board are paid their salaries by the respective organizations, are not conducive to careful, equitable consideration of the issues. The carriers' representatives insist that they are not "controlled" by the railroads and that they are capable of rendering decisions like any court of equity. Since they are not public officials, there is no reason to believe that, despite their protestations, the members can ignore their relationships to the parties involved in the grievance proceedings. The union representatives, of course, given their conception of the function of the Adjustment Board, recognize their allegiance to the unions. The bipartisan nature of the Board and the basic disagreement which exists as to its function and responsibility create an atmosphere of hostility among the members. These factors do not provide the proper background for the fair consideration of the issues.[29]

On the basis of the standards required of any grievance

procedure and in view of the discussion above, it would seem that the current grievance procedures in the railroad industry have broken down. This conclusion is reflected not only in the backlog of cases cited above, but also in the increasing number of strikes and threatened strikes in the railroad industry in the past few years over these issues. Some of these strikes have been due to disagreements between the parties on wages and working rules, the interpretations of which have laid the basis for many grievances. Other strikes have been called solely for the purpose of obtaining the settlement of grievances which have accumulated over a period of time. The National Mediation Board reports that during the fiscal year 1951 a total of twenty-four strikes were called against the railroads, the highest number reported since 1934.[30] These strikes for the most part involved operating workers, and a number were called primarily because the railroad labor organizations alleged that they could not obtain the settlement of their grievances. This problem has existed for many years.[31]

At this point it is appropriate to inquire into the causes for the failure of the grievance machinery in the railroad industry to settle disputes. It is suggested that the primary and basic cause is the fundamental conflict between the railroad labor organizations and the carriers over the working rules.

The Basic Conflict

The large backlog of cases, the large number of cases brought before the Adjustment Board, and the increasing number of strikes and threatened strikes over grievances, involving primarily the operating workers, reflect a basic conflict between the labor organizations and the carriers: the former seek not only the maintenance of the working rules by preventing any interpretation that might be adverse to railroad labor but also their extension regardless of the specific wording of the contract between the parties. The carriers, however, seek the elimination, or at least the modification, of the working rules.

The railroad unions, over the years, as indicated in Chapters III and IV, have been confronted with declining employment opportunities as a result of increasing competition among the various carriers of passengers and freight and the significant technological changes taking place in the railroad industry. Because of this threat to employment the railroad labor organizations have strongly resisted changes in the working rules. The impact is not simply one of lost jobs, but in many instances means the elimination of communities, which have grown up to service the railroads,[32] or the loss of seniority if the workers are forced to transfer to other places of employment. Thus the labor representatives on the Adjustment Board have been careful to avoid any "break" in the rules.

The railroads, however, insist that the working rules and their interpretation by the labor members of the Adjustment Board are a reflection of the "make-work" philosophy of the unions.[33] They insist that these rules result in higher direct costs and force the carriers to readjust their "practices in such a way as to be both more expensive and less efficient." [34] As pointed out in Chapter III, the carriers have in recent years sought extensive changes in the working rules.

This conflict between the parties is clearly revealed when one examines the arguments of each party in an attempt to explain the failure of the Adjustment Board. Both parties agree that the present procedure is defective.[35] The National Mediation Board concurs in this conclusion.[36]

The railroad labor organizations assert, first, that the railroads have refused to join the unions in the submission of cases to the board, thereby forcing the unions to submit ex parte cases.[37] The significance of the charge is that when a dispute is referred to the Adjustment Board by one party serious delays are encountered until the case is decided, since there may well be disagreement as to facts, and the gathering of the facts takes time.[38] It may be to the advantage of one of the parties to the dispute to delay a case. A second charge of the unions is that the railroads have refused to accept awards as precedent. This means that there is a succession of so-called "repeater" cases, that is, cases involving identical issues.[39] Since many of the awards involve the payment of money to the workers, based on the interpretation of the rules, the railroads obviously resist the final award.[40] And since these interpretations, if applied to many cases, might involve significant sums of money, the reason for the railroads' refusal to accept precedent is clear.[41] It is of no loss to the railroads to have each case argued before the Adjustment Board, while the unions bear the burden of waiting for a decision. And a large number of "repeater" cases clogs up the grievance machinery. A third complaint of the unions is that the carriers frequently refuse to accept the awards of the Board. If the carriers refuse to abide by the award, the union can secure enforcement by taking the case into court.[42] But the unions complain about the delay and the costs of bringing court action to enforce an award, which may involve a sum of money less than the court costs.[43] Instead, they have employed the threat of a strike as an alternative method of enforcement.[44] The basic charge of the unions is that there is considerable delay in the settlement of grievances and they imply that the railroads seek such delay.

The carriers have recognized that delay in the settlement of grievances has undermined the grievance system but have pointed to ways by which the situation can be improved. Such suggestions, in the eyes of the union, simply lay the foundation for modification of the working rules, if not their elimination. For example, the carriers point to the possibility of establishing regional or system boards.[45] The labor unions, however, are reluctant to accept this proposal because of the possibility that conflicting decisions may arise among the

BREAKDOWN OF GRIEVANCE PROCEDURES 149

boards, which might be an entering wedge for the elimination of the rules.[46] The carriers have recommended that the awards of the Adjustment Board be subject to court review, so that "firm principles" can be laid down by the courts.[47] The unions, however, are extremely reluctant to permit the courts, whom they consider "outsiders," to interpret working rules. Another recommendation of the carriers (concurred in by the National Mediation Board) is that permanent, rather than *ad hoc*, referees be appointed to expedite decisions, particularly since a significant number—about one third of the cases—are decided with the aid of a referee.[48] In view of the fact that the entire case has to be heard again when referred to a referee, the improvement in the procedure becomes obvious. But the unions have always been opposed to permanent referees, apparently fearful of any permanent official who could decide issues unfavorable to labor; they are also mindful of their experiences under the Railroad Labor Board.[49] The unions' attitude toward "outsiders" is clearly revealed in the 1951 controversy between the railroads and several railroad labor organizations. One of the obstacles to the settlement of the dispute was the refusal of the labor organizations to allow the President of the United States to select an arbitrator who would decide those rules questions on which the parties disagreed.[50] The Brotherhood of Railroad Trainmen did agree to submit four rules questions to an arbitrator, selected by the President. One of these awards resulted in the modification of the rule which required the payment of extra compensation for performing more than one class of service.[51] In transmitting a copy of this award to the membership an official of the Brotherhood of Locomotive Firemen and Enginemen, emphasizing the organization's opposition to the arbitration of the rules questions, urged each member to "notice the attitude and wording used"—which failed to appreciate the position of the union—as an "example of what may happen to us, if we ever agree to arbitrate the rules changes." [52]

It is apparent that the procedural difficulties which confront the Adjustment Board are nothing more than a reflection of the concern of the railroad labor organizations over the possible displacement of workers. The proposals made by the unions for the expedition of cases meet with the resistance of the carriers who are concerned with the continuing financial burdens of the rules. The proposals of the carriers, which would expedite cases, are opposed by the unions, who are fearful of the employment effects.[53]

SUGGESTIONS FOR THE IMPROVEMENT
OF GRIEVANCE PROCEDURES

The problem is not one susceptible of easy resolution because it reflects and arises out of the basic conflict between the carriers and the railroad unions. If not handled satisfactorily via the Adjustment Board, this conflict will naturally show up in other channels, namely in the form of strikes and threatened strikes or by the by-passing of the Adjustment Board and the seeking of a solution through the emergency board procedures of the Railway Labor Act. Nor are the emergency boards, whose members are not well versed in the intricacies and complexities of the working rules, equipped to handle such disputes.

Many suggestions have been made by those who have studied the problems confronting the National Railroad Adjustment Board. One group of suggestions has been concerned with the procedural aspects of the board's operations. Lloyd K. Garrison, for example, who has served as referee in many cases, has recommended first, that full-time referees be appointed; second, that a time limit be set within which railroad workers can file their claims; and third, that the procedure by which evidence is presented to the Board be improved.[54] Though these changes are desirable and intended to expedite the disposition of cases, they probably would not be acceptable to the labor organizations for reasons that have been discussed earlier.

A second group of suggestions has been concerned with the protection of individuals' rights before the Adjustment Board and was made as a result of two recent Supreme Court decisions which "conferred upon the NRAB exclusive primary jurisdiction of disputes involving the interpretation and application of collective bargaining agreements in the railroad industry." [55] In view of the bipartisan nature of the Adjustment Board, the tendency to indulge in "horse-trading" in the settlement of grievances, the virtual lack of representation of nonunion members before the Adjustment Board, the inability of claimants, who have been denied their claims, to appeal the decision to the courts, and the failure of the individual workers who are affected by the decisions of the Adjustment Board to have adequate notice and representation, it has been suggested that the Railway Labor Act be amended not only to eliminate these shortcomings but also to give all the participants—union members, nonunion members, and the carriers—in the proceedings an opportunity to have their cases adequately reviewed by the courts.[56]

Both sets of recommendations are commendable but fail to get at the root of the problem. The basic weakness of these and similar suggestions is that they take the working rules as given and seek improved methods for the settlement of grievances arising out of the interpretation and application of the rules. But given the basic conflict between the parties with respect to working rules and the reasons for such conflict, these suggested changes have little, if any, possibility of being enacted into legislation.

What must be achieved is the elimination or easing of many of the rules which, from a financial and economic point of view, are undesirable. This must be done, however, by agreement between the parties. It has been suggested that one way by which the railroad labor organizations might agree to the elimination of certain rules is to compensate the railroad workers for any financial losses involved, possibly in the form of increased wages.[57] But until the rules problem is resolved by mutual agreement between the parties there will continue to be in the railroad industry strikes and threatened strikes over grievance disputes.

CHAPTER XII

DEFECTS IN THE RAILWAY LABOR ACT

THE RAILROAD CARRIERS apparently are now convinced that the Railway Labor Act, as amended in 1934, has failed to achieve the objective as originally hoped for, namely, peaceful labor relations.[1] The reasons set forth by the officers of the carriers are two: It was originally hoped that the emergency boards' recommendations would marshal public opinion behind the decisions and bring about settlement on these terms, but such hopes have not materialized; the method by which disputes arising out of the interpretation of agreements are resolved has been unsatisfactory, as reflected in the large number of strikes which have developed out of these disputes and in the backlog of cases pending.[2]

The railroad unions, on the other hand, faced with the demand by the carriers for the revision of the Railway Labor Act so as to provide for compulsory arbitration of all labor disputes in the railroad industry and to eliminate strikes on the railroads, have attempted to minimize the defects of the law and have claimed that the railroads have refused to bargain collectively and have constantly sought the submission of disputes to emergency boards.[3]

Some students of the railroad labor problem have concluded that the basic fault in the law is the existence of the procedure itself: the establishment of emergency boards to hear evidence and to make their reports which are not binding on the parties.[4] Furthermore, as will be noted below, the long delays involved in the final settlement of railway labor disputes have not contributed toward stable labor relations. Finally, the long-drawn-out proceedings before emergency boards have, at times, muddied the issues and have not been helpful in assisting the boards in their determinations.

The arguments of the railroads and the unions set forth above, and the conclusions of the students of railroad labor relations will be examined in detail.

EMERGENCY BOARDS

The emergency board is nothing more than a final step in a series of procedures which the parties in a labor dispute, particularly one affecting the public interest, must follow. The original intent of both railway labor and management, in agreeing to such a procedure, was the same: namely, that "the parties to a dispute would voluntarily bow to the force of public opinion after a board had heard and studied the case and issued its report."[5] One railroad labor leader, in 1926, urged that the prestige of Presidential authority behind the report would bring about an amicable settlement of the labor dispute.[6] Yet the boards' recommendations in the past decade, in disputes involving national wage movements, have, with few exceptions, been rejected and the President has frequently seized the railroads. What have been the reasons for failure of emergency boards to settle disputes?

It has become obvious that the very existence of the emergency boards has completely broken down collective bargaining between the two parties. On the one hand, the railroad unions have, at times, entered the negotiations with the attitude that they can depend on their political power to obtain more than that offered by an emergency board or even by negotiations. Thus, the emergency boards' recommendations have become a springboard from which they could obtain further concessions. The events of the past decade confirmed this attitude, as the unions, at times, obtained more than the boards' recommendations in virtually every major case through the intervention of the President. Furthermore, the very existence of *ad hoc* boards permits union leaders to avoid responsibilities to their membership and gives them an opportunity to place the onus for the final outcome on an outsider.[7] Apparently, this was the experience of the National War Labor Board during World War II.[8] Some writers explain the wave of strikes in 1946, in part, in terms of the abandonment of collective bargaining as a means for the settlement of disputes during the war.[9]

On the other hand, railroad management has been accused of failing to bargain collectively and seeking an emergency board determination.[10] One union official alleged that "it is not until the emergency board has reported that any true, good faith collective bargaining can be expected from the carriers."[11] This attitude on the part of the carriers, the same official explained, "is prompted by the fear that when rate increases are sought from the Interstate Commerce Commission, their cases will be prejudiced if they have voluntarily entered into agreements with labor organizations which result in increased costs. The carriers feel that they must be forced into such cost increases by a government board recommendation."[12]

In general, experience with fact-finding in the settlement of industrial disputes has revealed that such procedure has not been particularly successful.[13] For, in most instances, the procedure has been imposed on the parties by the legislation. Yet, even when legislation is agreed upon between the two parties (as was the case under the Railway Labor Act), fact-finding has still not been successful. As Slichter has said: "The prospect that the government will appoint an emergency board is virtually an invitation to the parties not to settle their differences by bargaining or arbitration."[14]

In some instances, in recent years, fact-finding boards in other industries have been successful in mobilizing public opinion behind their recommendations and such procedure has been helpful in settling disputes.[15] And members of several such boards have been particularly hopeful about this method for the settlement of labor disputes, recognizing, at the same time, many of the difficulties involved.[16] But the significant difference between these cases and the railway cases lies in the fact that the boards created for the settlement of disputes in non-railroad industries have usually been established after the issues have been put forcefully before the public and, in some instance, after a strike. In the case of the railroads, the unions cannot strike until thirty days have elapsed after the issuance of the board's report and by that time the board's recommendations have been forgotten by the public.

The National Mediation Board has recently noted that "the machinery of the section 10 emergency boards has grown increasingly ineffective" and urged a revitalization of the procedure and a renewed respect for the recommendations of the emergency boards.[17]

To carry out this suggestion of the Board, it has been recommended by the chairman of the National Mediation Board that the President give support to emergency boards' recommendations by first, issuing a statement to the public as soon as the board's report is released; second, urging the acceptance of the recommendations, stating that the country could not stand a railroad strike; and third, urging both parties to cooperate with the National Mediation Board for the purpose of resolving the dispute within the framework of the board's recommendations.[18]

As the railroad unions have become more dissatisfied with the recommendations of emergency boards, as they have become increasingly aware of the restriction of their right to strike, and as they have found that Presidential intervention has been less of a help, they have been attempting to return to collective bargaining as a means of settling their labor disputes. But the railroads, for the same reasons, find it desirable to go to a board hearing (in addition to their need to obtain support for their demands for subsequent rate increases), and avoid collective bargaining. And this simply means that collective bargaining has virtually collapsed in the railroad industry.[19] Nor was the limitation of the right to strike via seizure and/or injunction an answer, for, as the National Mediation Board pointed out in reference to the 1948 seizure, such procedures "were effective in preventing the strike" but "they did not settle the dispute." [20]

Excessive Delays in the Settlement of Wage Disputes

The settlement of all types of labor disputes promptly and efficiently is essential for the maintenance of a spirit of genuine collective bargaining. In fact, delays in the settlement of the disputes reflect a serious breakdown in bargaining. And such delays in the settlement of disputes—those arising from the negotiation of new agreements (as well as grievances) —are typical of the railroad industry. The comment of one witness, who represented a CIO union which was also organizing railway workers, is of interest: "In one particular set of demands [involving a railroad], it took us eleven months to consummate an understanding. It is unbelievable. Some of the attitudes of railroad management are so different than the 1950 version of what good management attitude should be, as applied to outside industry, that when our organization first came on the railroads and started meeting with railroad management, we were utterly amazed. It was unbelievable. . . . The railroad industry today, in its attitude toward its employees, is literally years behind all other industries in the country." [21]

The facts with respect to delay are impressive. The most recent dispute between the railroads and the trainmen and conductors originated in March, 1949, and the emergency board decision was not issued until fifteen months later.[22] In its 1948 decision (March 27, 1948) an emergency board stated that "the issues before the board originated in 1945," although new issues were injected into the proceedings in September, 1947.[23] But this case was not finally settled—since the unions rejected the board's recommendations until August, 1948. The wage movements initiated during the summer and fall of 1945 were not finally settled until May, 1946, after emergency board hearings, seizure, and strikes.[24] In late 1942 and early 1943, the railroad unions began their movements for wage increases. Final settlement took place in January, 1944.[25]

What is the cause for these delays? Again, it reflects, to a large extent, a breakdown of collective bargaining procedures. The National Mediation Board has described the situation succinctly: "All of the national movements have shown a pattern of similarity, consisting of a uniform and national demand on the individual carriers; a perfunctory handling on both sides at the local level; the creation of national or regional carriers conference committees to meet the organizations on a national level; a breakdown of negotiations at this stage; mediation by the members of the National Mediation Board; inability to secure arbitration agreements; and finally, the setting of national strike dates and the consequent creation of emergency boards."[26] To this should be added, rejections of the boards' recommendations, strikes or threatened strikes, and further negotiations in the White House, either under government seizure or injunction. In other words, the very existence of the machinery under the Railway Labor Act may not only destroy collective bargaining (as noted previously), but may also provide the basis for delaying final settlement. Is there any reason to think that the railroads have a stake in avoiding collective bargaining and in seeking a hearing before an emergency board? First, the railroads may gain financially by delaying the initial payment of wage increases. Secondly, the standard procedure of the railroads has been to meet the proposals of the unions with counterproposals, usually involving a change in working rules. Presumably, the railroads hope to eliminate some of these rules—apparently a major objective. The unions, for reasons discussed previously, naturally reject the counterproposals. Therefore, the railroads always have a slim hope of eliminating some rules by arguing their unreasonableness before an emergency board. To date the railroads have not been too successful. The unions, to offset the counterproposals of the railroads, and in an attempt to extend the working rules, also inject demands for changes in rules into the proceedings.

The delays in the settlement of the labor disputes have brought unfavorable results to the railroad workers. In 1941, for example, while an emergency board was conducting hearings, the national wage stabilization policy was changed so as to disallow wage increases based on inequities. A more favorable decision for the workers might have come from the board—and the board did recognize the inequities—if the case had been decided earlier. Similarly, in periods of rapidly rising prices, the unions may discover that their original demands are inadequate to meet the change in the cost of living since the wage movement was initiated. In 1948, an emergency board noted in its report that "the organizations . . . stressed the fact that these proceedings are being carried on in 1948, and that the cost of living has risen substantially since September, 1947, when the employees' wage demands were submitted." But the board stated that it cannot "undertake consideration of anything like a third round of wage increases." [27]

Such long delays, which may involve a financial loss to the workers, are not a part of the process of genuine collective bargaining. And the existing machinery under the Railway Labor Act is a factor which gives the railroads an opportunity to postpone final settlement with possible benefits and no serious losses to themselves and possible harm to the unions whose members are concerned over the delays.

COMPLEXITY OF ISSUES PRESENTED TO EMERGENCY BOARDS

The hearings before the emergency boards have usually been lengthy and the issues presented numerous and complex. For example, one hearing extended for six weeks, and the transcript consisted of 5,253 pages of testimony and 123 exhibits.[28] And this is not an unusual case. What are the reasons for such lengthy hearings?

Again, the answer to this question is found in a "lack of thorough exploration and negotiation on the many issues." [29] And this stems from the basic conflict between the unions and the railroads on working rules, which are the basic cause for the length of the hearings. As one board noted, it was, in effect, given the task of writing a complete agreement involving intricate rules which are only understood by persons intimately connected with the industry.[30] The boards, in this case and in others, were not resolving questions of principle, but were made (in the words of one board) "the target for a barrage of conflicting arguments about a lot of little details." [31]

Aside from the problem of attempting to resolve conflicts over complex working rules, which have bogged down the proceedings, the boards are consistently confronted with a series of problems which are statistical in nature. And these problems are constantly reargued before the board. A few illustrations are in order. In every case, the emergency board is faced with the choice of accepting data presented by unions or the railroads, each of whom computes the data differently. In the computation of average hourly earnings should hours "not worked but paid for" be included? The unions say yes —since it reduces the average—the railroads say no—since it raises the average. Should the five cents awarded operating workers in 1943 in lieu of overtime and other expenses be included in the base rate? Again, the two groups disagree.

DEFECTS IN THE ACT

In comparing railroad wages with wages in other industries, which "other" industries should be included? And should one use hourly rates, hourly earnings, weekly earnings, or annual earnings? All these questions are discussed, analyzed, and debated before each board. And instead of the board's being faced with a question of resolving principle, it is faced—in addition to resolving complex issues concerning rules—with conflicting testimony and evidence.

At one hearing the writer attended, the railroad union offered to present its case in a week and stated positively that it was interested in resolving a question of principle and not questions of detail. Humorously, the railroad attorney remarked that he hoped the union would be able to present as good a case as other unions involved. But the offer to submit a case on principle was apparently not taken seriously by the railroad nor by the board. In any event, the railroad indicated its need for more time than one week.

Thus, the combination of complex rules and intricate statistical data must, perforce, cause considerable confusion and doubt in the minds of the board members. And to fill a record with this kind of material fails to assist in the resolution of the labor dispute.

The rules problem goes deep. Its resolution is not simple. But the statistical questions might be resolved by stipulation between the parties.

Part III: Strikes Affecting the Public Interest

CHAPTER XIII

THE RIGHT OF RAILROAD WORKERS TO STRIKE

ON THE ISSUE of the right of railroad workers to strike, there is sharp disagreement among various students of labor, as well as officials at various levels of government activity. Three schools of thought exist. One group insists that the right to strike should not be limited, either because compulsion of any sort will not work or because of a belief in the absolute right of workers to strike, regardless of the essentiality of the industry. Another group urges that public interest is paramount and, in those industries which are essential to the public welfare, the right to strike cannot be absolute. Under these circumstances it follows that special procedures must be developed for the settlement of labor disputes in these industries. A third group, however, thinks that strikes as such cannot be prevented, even if forbidden by law, and that any compulsive procedure established to resolve a labor dispute in an essential industry would only lead to more disputes. The sole solution, according to this group, lies in the establishment of procedures which would bring about a resolution of the labor dispute on a voluntary basis—e.g., mediation and conciliation—without any "coercive intervention" by the government.

With respect to the issue of the right to strike, the discussion which follows will consider the problem in terms of the following questions:
1. Is there an absolute right to strike?
2. What effect does the denial of the right to strike have on collective bargaining?
3. What has been the experience when this right has

been abrogated, both in the United States and abroad?
4. What are the implications of the abrogation of this right?

In Defense of the Right to Strike

At the outset it should be noted that there is no disagreement that under the thirteenth amendment to the Constitution of the United States no individual worker can be forced to work involuntarily. A worker has the right to *quit* his job. The issue is whether a worker can leave his job, in concert with others, and still keep a vested interest in the job. It might be noted, in passing, that under certain specific conditions, even the right to quit a job is not absolute. For example, "it is a criminal offense for train crews to abandon a train at a time, and under circumstances endangering human life." [1] But, essentially, the right of a railroad worker to quit his job is set forth in the Railway Labor Act, as amended:

Nothing in the Act shall be construed to require an individual employee to render labor or service without his consent, nor shall anything in this Act be construed to make quitting of his labor or service by an individual employee an illegal act; nor shall any court issue any process to compel the performance by an individual employee of such labor or service, without his consent.[2]

It is clear that this right does not, in the words of Donald Richberg, one of the co-framers of the Railway Labor Act of 1926, "have any reference to group action." [3]

The position of the unions on the right to strike has been consistent, but not necessarily correct on legal grounds. The AF of L's position has generally been that to prohibit strikes is a violation of the Constitution, particularly the thirteenth amendment.[4] Although the unions recognize the distinction between voluntary quitting and concerted action to strike, they urge, first, that in "our twentieth century industrial economy . . . individual quittings are but hopeless gestures," and, second, that it is virtually impossible to make a distinction between quitting and striking.[5] However, over the years the courts have repeatedly refused to accept the right to strike as being absolute. The Supreme Court in one case stated that "neither the common law, nor the fourteenth amendment, confers the absolute right to strike." [6] This language was again accepted by the court in a more recent case.[7]

If the argument is accepted that there is no absolute right to strike under the Constitution, then several questions naturally arise: should the legislature give the workers the absolute right to strike or should it expressly forbid the right to strike under certain specified conditions? And, if the latter course is taken, under what conditions should the denial of the right to strike prevail? And, finally, what machinery should be established to enforce such a law?

Aside from the legality of the right to strike, many persons from all sections of American life have resisted any curtailment of the right to strike. The arguments fall basically into three categories: that any denial of the right to strike destroys the process of collective bargaining; that the denial may threaten the destruction of a free enterprise economy; that experience has demonstrated that such denials have been ineffective.

If the right to strike is taken away from a group of workers, the law must provide for methods for the resolution of a labor dispute. One method is compulsory arbitration, a method adopted by several states. A second method, employed in recent years by the federal government, has been seizure and eventual settlement either by further negotiation between the government and the workers (as in the United Mine Workers case) or by further negotiation between the parties under the aegis of the White House.

With respect to the effect of compulsory arbitration on

collective bargaining, the argument has been put neatly by George W. Taylor who said:

The evidence strongly indicates . . . that the mere provision for ultimate compulsory arbitration in itself discourages the making of those offers and counter-offers without which there is no negotiation. Why should the employer make any offer which the union may use, not as a starting point for agreement, but as a springboard for arbitration? Why should a union accept any employer offer when, in compulsory arbitration, it would not likely get less and might get more? Why shouldn't a union make and hold to a large number of so-called "fringe" demands? If they are dismissed in arbitration, nothing has been lost. If they are approved, much is gained. Negotiating tactics are almost certain to be entirely different when compulsory arbitration, and not a strike, is the last step. The reason: Under collective bargaining a dispute can only be settled by a meeting of minds; in compulsory arbitration this criterion is removed.[8]

Would the effect on collective bargaining relationships be the same if seizure were provided for as an alternative to compulsory arbitration? Taylor thinks that under such procedure the final settlement of the dispute would be achieved either by the government's mediating the dispute or actually negotiating an agreement directly with the union. If mediation is the procedure followed, he says, "Government seizure need not vitiate the collective bargaining criterion of the meeting of the minds." But if the government negotiates the agreement the employer is deprived of his collective bargaining rights.[9]

It seems to this writer that either method of resolving a dispute after seizure by the government may destroy collective bargaining. In the case of the railroad industry, specifically, it has been stated previously that, in essence, the recommendations of an emergency board would be the basis of final settlement of a dispute after seizure, with the government mediating the dispute. Knowing that the right to strike is denied to railroad workers, is there any reason to believe that the railroads would bargain collectively with the unions? It would appear to be of benefit to the carriers to run the gamut of the procedures, as discussed in detail earlier.[10] On the other hand, if the railroad unions and the carriers knew that eventual agreement would have to be reached by negotiation between the workers and the government, why should the unions accept the carriers' final offer? And why should the railroads make any concessions? It would seem that the seizure procedure, and subsequent settlement either as a result of mediation or as a result of agreement between the workers and the government, would be as destructive of the process of collective bargaining as compulsory arbitration.

In several states in the United States, and in some foreign countries, the general method for prohibiting strikes in industries affecting the public interest has been, and is, compulsory arbitration. How successful has such procedure been? As one writer has said: "Compulsory arbitration doesn't eliminate strikes; it makes them illegal." [11] This conclusion has been confirmed by studies made of foreign as well as American experience.

With respect to foreign experience—particularly in Australia and New Zealand—it has been found that, despite the existence of compulsory arbitration, work stoppages "have occurred regardless of their legality or illegality." [12] Similar conclusions have been drawn by other investigators.[13]

An analysis of the domestic experience has revealed the same results. In 1920 the state of Kansas established a court of industrial relations which had the power to settle all labor controversies in industries affected by the public interest.[14] The applicability of the compulsory arbitration machinery to manufacturing and transportation industries was declared unconstitutional and the court was abolished in 1925.[15] It is interesting to note that, in the opinion of one writer, "efforts to evaluate the experience of the state of Kansas . . . has indicated by and large that the experiment was not successful, measured in terms of strike activity." [16]

Since 1947 eleven states have enacted legislation providing for compulsory arbitration, seizure, or both, in public utility labor disputes.[17] Although it is premature to make a complete evaluation of these statutes, certain evidence is beginning to appear which would seem to indicate that this recent domestic experience has been similar to the foreign experience. For example, one writer has asserted that after four years of experience under the New Jersey statute "strikes have continued to occur. Whether there have been more or fewer than would have occurred is debatable." [18] The study revealed that in one instance a company and a union had been able to settle their differences without a strike or lockout for twenty-four years, but in 1947, the first year of operation of the New Jersey law, the parties were unable to agree.[19]

Another recent study of compulsory arbitration of utility disputes in New Jersey and Pennsylvania indicates that in New Jersey the very existence of the procedures may have, in some industries, "restricted or injured collective bargaining." [20] This conclusion was based on an analysis of the disputes in the state from April, 1947, to March, 1951. During this period, approximately 24 percent of the negotiations resulted in seizures or stipulations to arbitrate. For the country as a whole, the percentage was about 5 percent. The analysis of the operations of the Pennsylvania statute did not lead to any definite conclusions with respect to the effect of compulsory arbitration upon collective bargaining because the number of cases was limited and both sides apparently avoided the use of the provisions of the law.

Another argument put forth by those who oppose compulsory arbitration is that if wage and working conditions are controlled it would be essential that some consideration be given to the control over prices charged by the industry involved. Such an argument has been put forth by labor, management, and disinterested parties.[21] It is true that in the railroad industry the prices are also controlled by a governmental agency, but Senator Morse, who not only has had considerable experience in the general field of industrial relations, but also has been a member of an emergency board under the Railway Labor Act, has pointed out how important it was that the group which had responsibility for the establishment of the wage rates should also be empowered to set prices.[22]

Those persons who insist that workers have an absolute right to strike—even in essential industries—urge that "injury to the public, while regrettable, is as much a necessary by-product in industrial welfare as it is in wars among nations." [23] What is implied by this statement is that if the right to strike is considered a basic liberty essential to our democracy, we should be willing to pay the cost of a strike just as we are willing to pay the cost of a war in defense of our other liberties. This argument, of course, goes beyond the legal basis for a strike and becomes a question of morality. One might go further and urge that the free organization of workers and completely free collective bargaining are not only fundamental to democracy, but also a bulwark in the defense of democracy. Therefore, despite the immediate cost of any strike, the weakening of the trade unions may result in an even greater loss in the long run. But such an argument can be neither proved nor disproved by facts; it is essentially a reflection of a judgment "on balance." Nonetheless, it should be carefully considered in weighing the "gains" and "losses" in the denial of the right to strike, even in an essential industry like the railroads.

There are some who think that this denial should apply only to essential industries. But what is an essential industry? And even if a strike does occur in an essential industry, is an emergency automatically created? The courts, and state officials as well, have disagreed on just what an emergency is.[24] We have seen public utilities struck, but the service still forthcoming.[25]

A study of the impact of bituminous coal strikes in recent years reveals that they did not create any national emergencies, at least for the time during which the coal mines were shut down.[26] Strikes on railroads and bus transportation systems do, of course, create considerable inconvenience, but neither public health nor safety will necessarily break down.[27] Apparently what labor and others fear is a gradual whittling down of the right to strike once such right is denied to one group of workers.[28] In the case of the railroad industry, how widespread a work stoppage is necessary before such stoppage affects the public interests? Can it be measured in numbers? Surely not, because a small group of switchmen might have strategic control over a railroad yard in an important railroad junction. If one railroad is struck, is this work stoppage affecting the public interest? What if the nonoperating workers strike? Are they, by stopping work, affecting the public interest? These questions indicate the difficulty of deciding whether or not the public interest is affected, even in the railroad industry. And if the workers and the carriers do not have, while negotiating, a clearcut knowledge of their bargaining strength, the collective bargaining procedure will be adversely affected.

In Opposition to the Right to Strike

Those who advocate the denial of the right to strike in industries whose closing down would "gravely jeopardize the public health, the public safety, or the general welfare," do so on the basis that the need for continuous service is paramount to the right to strike.[29] In such instances, it is urged, "it, of course, is essential that the government have adequate authority and well-planned policies to protect the community against strikes and lockouts." [30] It has been suggested by one careful observer that the right to strike is, today, an economic anachronism. He states that the strike weapon, which was suitable as a labor counterpoise in a small-scale capitalistic economy, is becoming obsolescent in a modern economy in which institutional continuity of operation is of the essence.[31]

If the right to strike is denied, it is, of course, essential that certain machinery be adapted to meet the problem if and when it arises. A variety of suggestions have been made and these will be discussed below.

One technique, adopted by several states in handling public utility disputes, is compulsory arbitration after certain procedures such as cooling-off periods, fact-finding board decisions, and mediation, have been followed. The extent to which this procedure is effective has been described above.

An alternative method is seizure by the public authority.[32] What is meant by "seizure," according to one writer, is simply "the taking of possession by the government, of a business for the purpose of securing its continued operation during the period of a labor dispute." It does not imply government ownership nor does it imply government operation. The workers, however, acquire the status of government employees and become subject to the limitation of the right to strike on the part of government workers in general. The extent to which the government actually operates the property or simply supervises it depends upon the executive order or statute under which seizure takes place.[33]

In the case of the railroads, seizure itself was not always effective, since, in a few instances—as in the 1948 and 1950 cases—injunctions had to be obtained to prevent or stop the strikes. And in the 1950 case, we have observed the violation of the injunction itself and subsequent successful contempt proceedings.

Why, particularly in the case of the railroads, has seizure itself not been completely successful in avoiding strikes? The unions (particularly the railroad unions) have objected to this method and therefore resisted it chiefly on two grounds: First, the seizure was simply formal and did not actually result in government operation; therefore, the railroad worker may be a government worker *de jure*, but not *de facto*.[34] Second, the unions have urged that if the worker is to be denied the right to strike by seizure and/or injunction, the profits of the railroads should be taken by the government during the period of seizure.[35] Thus, in a few instances the unions forced the government to obtain court injunctions to prevent a strike and in some cases even attempted to avoid the injunction by calling "sick" strikes.

On the question of whether or not the railroad worker, under conditions of government seizure, is actually a government worker, the unions have pointed out, in part, that after seizure the Secretary of the Army has refused to bargain with the union and actually urged that the railroad unions continue to bargain with the carriers.[36] The question of retention of profits also raises many difficult problems. The union insists that, since "the carriers cannot possibly lose financially, but rather gain additional profits as long as they can deprive their employees of just changes in wages, rules, and working conditions" there is no "influence on the American railroads to encourage settlement of labor disputes." [37]

The first question is, of course, one to be decided by the courts—whether "token" seizure brings about a change in the status of railroad workers, and therefore exempts them from the injunction provisions of the Norris–La Guardia Act. In a concurring opinion in the United Mine Workers case, two justices stated that "if we thought . . . that the government's possession and operation of the mines were not genuine, but merely pretended, we should then say that the Norris–La Guardia Act barred these proceedings. For anything less than full and complete government operation for its own account would make this proceeding the equivalent of the government's seeking an injunction for the benefit of the private employers. We think the Norris–La Guardia Act prohibits that." [38]

A far more serious question involved in the issue of employee status is that of the sanctions to be imposed in case there is a violation of the injunction.[39] During wartime, sanctions employed in other industries including the drafting of workers into the armed forces, the use of troops to break strikes, "the withholding of awards, the withholding of labor union rights, the withholding of individual rights, and the legal prosecution of individual strike leaders." [40] In the railroad industry two techniques have been employed: one involved contempt proceedings against the union as such and the imposition of a fine for violating the injunction. This may prove to be effective because of the unions' unusually large assets which stem from their insurance activities.[41] A second method, employed recently, was a threat by the Secretary of the Army that unless the striking workers returned to their jobs by a certain date, they would be "fired" and lose all their employee rights, including seniority.[42] The strike ended immediately. However, an interesting question would arise if all railroad workers refused to return to work. How would the railroads run? And if, as in 1946, the President asked Congress for legislation to empower him to draft railroad workers into the Army, and if such legislation were enacted (the House of Representatives actually passed the legislation), what if the workers still refused to return to work? [43]

On the basis of recent experience on the railroads one may conclude that, though seizure, injunctions, contempt proceedings, fines, and government threats may prevent strikes, they do not settle labor disputes. They must still be settled by negotiation between the parties. And, it may well be, that the very existence of the seizure procedure breaks down collective bargaining in the first instance. Furthermore, seizure tends to give management greater power in collective bargaining.

A Senate committee, investigating the 1950–1951 dispute between the railroads and four operating brotherhoods, pointed out in its report that government seizure may have been more helpful to management and of no assistance to railroad labor because the railroads continued to be operated by the same railroad officials under the general direction of the Army. "Under the organizational set-up actually established, the railroad employees could not help but feel . . . that Government policies and decisions were simply those of management, further armed with the power of Government. This feeling, in turn, could not help but prejudice the prospects for an early settlement of the strike by negotiations between the brotherhoods and the carriers, and thus enable the Government to end its seizure." [44] In other words, the pressure is on the unions to come to an agreement, and management stands little to lose as long as the railroads are under government control. The Senate committee's report stated further, that "Government seizure which protects the position of one of the parties as against that of the other, unfairly relieves that party of the necessity to continue good faith negotiations and collective bargaining." [45]

The language of the report of the Senate committee is mild compared to a preliminary report of the same committee which was circulated but finally revised. An examination of this report reveals that the committee concluded that "Government . . . operation is a token operation" because the same personnel is running the railroads. Comparing the operation of the railroads under private management and under government control, the committee noted that "the only difference . . . is that under seizure, railroad management has been vested with the power and prestige of the Federal Government. In other words, railroad management, having failed to reach agreement with their employees through orderly procedures of collective bargaining, Government seizure has the effect that the same railroad management can now impose its will by the very power of the Government itself." [46]

The general practice with respect to the profits of the railroads while under government seizure has been to negotiate an agreement with the railroads so that the government would not be responsible for paying the railroads the amount of profit which the railroads would have earned were it not for the seizure, and, conversely, the government would not be responsible for any of the operating losses.[47] The question of whether or not the government can negotiate such agreement is still uncertain, and it may well be that at some future date the railroads may receive payment for any losses suffered because of government seizure.[48] In a recent case involving the government seizure of a coal mine, the Supreme Court awarded the company a payment for the losses incurred during the period of government ownership and operation, disregarding the issue of whether or not the losses under private ownership might have been the same or greater.[49] In this case the Court held that the government ownership and control was complete. It is possible that the issue of whether the government actually owned and controlled the railroads in recent seizures might influence the Court's decision. In any event, there is still some doubt as to the government's liability when the railroads are seized.

The effect of the seizure procedure is to guarantee the income of the railroads, with no sacrifice to the railroads as a result of seizure, while the workers continue to receive the wages in effect at the time of seizure. Thus, the railroads would have little to lose and might well gain by forcing the dispute to run the gamut of the procedures as outlined in the Railway Labor Act and as extended by the White House. Thus, if one were seeking to avoid any favoritism with respect to seizure, some device must be found which would make it financially undesirable for either side to seek ultimately the seizure of the property.

An interesting plan has been suggested by one student of the problem.[50] It is proposed that "the principles of the law of eminent domain" be applied. Under this principle, the government would take possession of the railroad, for example, and on the basis of an investigation of a fact-finding commission would determine "just compensation" both for the workers and for the company. In other words, the company would be simply limited to "the fair rental value of its property" and the extra profits, if any, would revert to the Treasury Department. One serious problem in the application of this plan, aside from its constitutionality, to the railroad industry is the strong possibility that the earning power or profits of the railroads may not be adversely affected, given the present method of calculating rates of return.

To meet this objection, one might consider an alternative proposal by two economists who suggest a scheme whereby both parties would suffer losses equivalent to those which would have been sustained if an actual strike had taken place.[51] Under the plan "the workers would receive a rate so low that, in actual fact, they would be under the same economic pressure that a strike would exert." [52] Further, "the company would be required to pay out (for all work performed) at a rate so high that the company would stand in the same profit and loss position in which it would have stood had the work stoppage gone ahead." This type of strike is called by the proponents of the plan a "statutory strike," which would go into effect whenever the President declares it to be applicable. Certain objections—such as the constitutionality of the plan, its effectiveness, the degree of compliance possible, and the extent to which it penalizes both sides sufficiently to induce a settlement—can be raised against the plan. But these objections can be raised against virtually every plan. The merit of the proposal lies in the fact that the device is such as to make it unattractive for either party to force seizure for its own benefit and therefore it meets the fundamental objection to all proposals of this type—namely, that the procedure itself destroys collective bargaining.

Alternative Proposals

A third group—and this includes the Congress of the United States—recognizes the seriousness of a strike in an essential industry but at the same time is reluctant to deny (by legislation) to the workers the right to strike. But a careful analysis of their position reveals that, though they refuse to deny a worker or a group of workers the right to strike by legislative means, they recognize that if the strike would paralyze the nation, the President would step in and "do something about it."

William Green, testifying before a Congressional committee which was considering compulsory arbitration for the railroad industry, said that in "an emergency" the President would have the inherent power to "step in and interfere" with a strike.[53] Similarly, the Secretary of Labor stated that he was opposed to any denial of the right to strike among workers in essential industries, but he admitted that "no President of the United States is ever going to permit the economy of the United States to be brought to its knees."[54] A well-known lawyer and labor arbitrator, William H. Davis, put it colorfully when he stated that if the railroads are shut down, "the President will do what the President has always done. He will come in and keep the railroads running." Thus, each time we have had an emergency in our history, "we have had a President with the courage to act and save the Union—usually unconstitutionally or extra-constitutionally. Then after the Union is saved and the emergency is over, the thing gets into the Supreme Court and they say the thing is unconstitutional and thereby save the Constitution."[55]

Similarly, Congress has refused to deny the right to strike to workers in essential industries. Under the Taft-Hartley Law (Section 208–210) provision is made for a so-called "cooling-off" period, the creation of fact-finding boards, and the issuance of injunctions to prevent strikes during the period when the procedures under the law are followed.[56] But after a period of about ninety days has elapsed, the injunction against the strike lapses, and the President is directed to report to Congress and make appropriate recommendations. To date we have not had any case reach the point where the President has made recommendations to Congress and so one has no experience to make any judgment on this part of the Taft-Hartley Law. There is, however, some evidence that the entire procedure itself has not been particularly effective.[57]

During the debate in Congress on the so-called "national emergencies" provisions of the Taft-Hartley Law, even Senator Taft was specific in pointing out that free collective bargaining must be maintained and in emergencies "Congress can pass an emergency law to cover the particular emergency." [58]

Thus, we have agreement among various groups that the right to strike should not be specifically denied, even to workers in essential industries. The reason for the position of labor is clear: it not only needs this right to match its power with that of the employer, but it also fears a "whittling" away of the right. Congressional aversion may well be attributed to political considerations. But to students of labor, the great fear is that if both sides *know* beforehand what the *specific* procedure will be in case of a stalemate in collective bargaining, one side or the other will find it attractive to invoke the procedure and, in the words of one student of labor, "there goes your collective bargaining." [59]

Thus, this last group seeks a strengthening of the mediation and conciliation activities of governmental bodies since, in its view, under voluntary methods, collective bargaining may be advanced, while under compulsion—procedurally or otherwise—collective bargaining is retarded.[60] One well-known student of this problem concluded his analysis of the problem of governmental intervention in labor disputes by stating that "a democratic government must be very careful not to expose its own impotence." [61]

Conclusion

It would appear that workers in essential industry can probably be prevented from striking, by legal or extralegal means. Or at least the number of strikes may be minimized. But such compulsion does not resolve the dispute and may virtually destroy collective bargaining. Labor contends that the denial of this right deprives it of its sole weapon in bargaining with management and that any method designed to resolve the problem simply hurts the union but not the company. Management—though this is not true of railroad management—fears compulsion because it might lead to other controls, a fear, incidentally, with which railroad management need not concern itself because it is already subject to regulation. Many students of labor oppose compulsion because the procedures established tend to destroy collective bargaining.

Part IV: Conclusion

CHAPTER XIV

SUMMARY AND RECOMMENDATIONS

DURING the past decade the problem of strikes, threatened strikes, the issuance of court injunctions, and government seizures, has arisen in the railroad industry. The problem is particularly acute in view of the role that railroad transportation plays in our economy both in peace and in war. In view of the fact that the Railway Labor Act, as amended, provides for certain orderly procedures in the settlement of all labor disputes in the railroad industry, an explanation of the unstable labor relations in that industry and an evaluation of the law is in order.

In Chapters II–V there is a discussion of the railroad industry; a description of employment, method of wage payments, and working rules of the railroad workers; a summary of the labor organizations in the industry; and a history of governmental intervention in railway labor disputes. From this discussion it is found, first, that in the railroad industry most of the freight and passenger traffic is handled by a relatively small number of railroads and passes through a handful of railroad terminals. This means that the railroad labor organizations can easily disrupt the transportation system of the United States by striking certain railroads or terminals. It is suggested that the financial position of the railroads and the procedures established by the Interstate Commerce Commission for the determination of rates are such that the railroads find themselves in a position whereby they are unable to agree across the table to demands for wage increases. In periods of depression, because of the competitive situation in the transportation industry, the railroads cannot afford to raise their rates. They must look for lower costs. Wage cuts are resisted and any attempt to lower expenses by consolidating railroads is usually strongly resisted by the labor organizations. On the other hand, when the railroads seek higher rates during periods of great economic activity—when the competitive factor is minimized—the Interstate Commerce Commission has usually been reluctant to grant such increases because the revenue seems to be adequate at that time in view of the greater volume of traffic. And during the latter period the railroads apparently feel that to get a rate increase as a result of a wage increase it is essential that they demonstrate to the Commission that they resisted the wage increase as much as possible. In other words, any acquiescence to an increase in wages in the early stages of negotiation might weaken their case before the Commission. Because of the financial position of the railroads, a program of mechanization has been initiated, which is a threat to the employment of the workers in the industry. The impact of the mechanization program on employment has resulted in a demand on the part of labor for a continuation and extension of working rules so as to counteract the employment effects and the threat to the labor organizations themselves.

A description of the labor organizations is also set forth in these chapters, revealing a background of militancy and interunion conflicts. These conditions are not very conducive to peaceful labor relations.

Finally, a survey of the history of governmental intervention in railway labor disputes is presented, going back as far as 1888, when the first of such legislation was enacted, and certain patterns are revealed. It is found, for example, that compulsion of any sort usually proved unsuccessful and that mediation and voluntary arbitration were most successful in the settlement of labor disputes. In addition, both parties to the disputes have frequently switched their attitudes toward governmental intervention and have acted in an opportunistic manner. Furthermore, the economic and social conditions of the period and the economic and social status of the workers, rather than the provisions of the law itself, played important roles in the success or failure of the legislation. And, finally, adequate provisions for the settlement of disputes arising out of the interpretation and application of collective bargaining agreements were essential to labor peace.

With this as a background, Chapters VI–XII are concerned with the causes of the breakdown of the Railway Labor Act, as amended. It is suggested that, although the record—based on the number and extent of strikes in the railroad industry, as compared with the rest of industry, and the mediation record of the National Mediation Board—seems, at first glance, rather impressive, a careful analysis raises some doubts. A survey of the concerted wage and rules movements during the past ten years reveals that most of these disputes were settled by running the gamut of procedures not only set forth in the Railway Labor Act, as amended, but also improvised by Presidential intervention, court injunctions, and government seizures. How does one explain the virtual collapse of collective bargaining between the parties and the lack of success of the procedures set forth in the Act? First, the economic position of the railroad workers has, over the years, deteriorated when measured in terms of their relative wage position. This is particularly true of the operating workers, who have been involved in most of the serious strikes and threatened strikes in the railroad industry. These workers no longer are the "aristocrats of labor." This deterioration, it is shown, is to a large extent explained by the fact that the emergency boards, which are established under the law by the President, have not followed any consistent, objective set of standards for the purpose of wage determination. The relatively lower wage position of the railroad workers is also explained by the fact that we have had compulsory arbitration, *de facto* but not *de jure*, in the railroad industry. This condition developed as a result of Presidential intervention, government seizures, and the issuance of court injunctions, thereby depriving the workers of their sole economic weapon in collective bargaining. Such compulsion naturally places the workers in an inferior bargaining position not only with the railroads, but also before the emergency boards.

Second, aside from the deterioration of the position of the railroad workers, there has been a virtual breakdown of the grievance procedures as set forth in the Act. The breakdown arises essentially from a basic conflict between the parties: the unions seek to maintain and extend the rules because of their security drive, while the railroads attempt to revise and eliminate them because of the direct and indirect costs involved. The procedures themselves have broken down because the parties disagree as to the function of the National Railroad Adjustment Board, the unions claiming that the Board is nothing more than an agency where the parties continue to negotiate and the carriers suggesting that the Board should act more like a court of equity. As a result of this conflict, a large backlog of cases has accumulated and the unions have turned to the strike or threatened strike in order to obtain a settlement of their grievances.

Third, it is urged that the very existence of the Railway Labor Act itself prevents the establishment of a spirit of genuine collective bargaining. As long as procedures exist for the resolution of a dispute, it is natural for one or both parties to think that they could obtain a better result by utilizing the procedure. Furthermore, the procedure itself, as it has developed, results in excessive delays in the final settlement of the disputes, and such delays do not make for peaceful labor relations. Finally, the proceedings before the emergency boards are usually long and extended, as complex issues and facts are presented and argued by both sides. The result is a burden on the members of the emergency boards—most of whom are not specialists—and a great deal of confusion about the real issues involved.

SUMMARY AND RECOMMENDATIONS

Given this explanation for the large number of strikes and threatened strikes on the railroad industry, the problem still remains. What to do? Chapter XII is concerned with this question. It is suggested that there are three main approaches to the problem of strikes in industries which the public considers so essential to the health and welfare of the community. One group urges that the right to strike should not in any way be curtailed. This position derives either from an attitude that compulsion of any sort is never successful, or from an attitude that the long-run implications of the elimination of the right to strike are such as to offset any short-term gains. A second group denies that workers in essential industries should have the right to strike. The problem facing this group is to devise a scheme whereby the denial of the right to strike is balanced by some sort of penalty to management. Such proposals are discussed and analyzed. A third group, though recognizing the problem of strikes in essential industries, would prefer that no procedures be set up for the handling of such situations, but rather that there exist an air of uncertainty as to what will happen if such strike does occur. This position is based on the attitude that procedures themselves destroy collective bargaining, that the government has inherent powers to act when necessary, and that Congress can act quickly during an emergency.

On the basis of this analysis, it becomes clear that any attempt to meet the problem by making minor adjustments in the Railway Labor Act, as amended, must, of necessity, fail because they do not go to the roots of the conflict.

A basic theme of this discussion is that laws do not prevent strikes, they simply make them illegal. Therefore, the solution is not the banning of strikes, but the restoration of conditions under which genuine collective bargaining between the two parties can be carried on. It has been frequently suggested throughout the course of the study that, as long as specific procedures exist for the resolution of disputes which cannot be resolved through collective bargaining, such procedures themselves destroy collective bargaining.

And this presents the nation with a basic conflict. Can the country stand aside and make *no* provision for the resolution of labor disputes in essential industries when the parties themselves cannot agree? Or should the force of government be applied which would have the result of depriving the workers of their sole economic weapon—the strike? On the one hand it appears that the government is impotent. On the other hand, such compulsion may be the first inroad into our basic freedoms. Or must we agree that our highly advanced, complex, and closely integrated economic system can no longer allow for really free collective bargaining?

Recommendations

To accept the latter conclusion is to acknowledge our inability to meet the problems of a complex society within a democratic framework. It would be to deny our ingenuity and ability to solve the problem. It is too early to abandon the search for a solution.

To accept compulsion and to deny the railroad worker the right to strike means that a retreat on one front may well result in a retreat on another. It is fairly easy to begin to define many industries as essential, and with that we begin to accept the incompatibility of our technology and our freedoms. But if we do deny the right of the railroad workers to strike, it is essential that every attempt be made to assure workers a wage equivalent to that which they would have received under free collective bargaining. To deny them this is to impose on one group of workers certain obligations without any compensation.

But the basic objection to either approach is that each fails to meet the real problems. Further, in the opinion of the writer, whatever the cost of actual strikes might be to society

SUMMARY AND RECOMMENDATIONS

—in the form of effects on public health and welfare—the eventual cost of government compulsion may be greater. Therefore, the following recommendations are offered for *reducing* the conflict between railroad carriers and railroad labor:

1. The provision of the Railway Labor Act, as amended, with respect to the creation of emergency boards, should be eliminated. As has been suggested in the course of the discussion, such procedure tends to discourage collective bargaining because either party might think that it can obtain greater returns from the utilization of the procedure. If emergency boards continue to be employed as part of the procedure for the settlement of disputes, the parties should agree to the establishment of certain objective principles for wage determination and to the elimination of many extraneous issues from the proceedings.
2. The mediation and conciliation activities of the National Mediation Board should be extended and this method of settling labor disputes should be emphasized. Experience has shown this method to be most satisfactory.
3. The law should remain silent on what the country will do in case of a strike or threatened strike. The uncertainty would make each side extremely cautious in avoiding a responsibility for bargaining in good faith.
4. If, and when, a strike does occur on a railroad, and prior to any seizure or to the issuance of any injunction, the President should make a determination, by any means he sees fit, of first, the issues in the case, and second, whether or not the public health and welfare are involved. If it is determined that an emergency will exist or does exist, then the President should take appropriate action, but the action should not be known prior to the breakdown of negotiations, nor should it be such as to hurt unduly one party as compared to the other party to the dispute.
5. With respect to grievances arising out of the interpretation

of agreements, action along the following lines should be taken:

a. Make procedural changes to hasten the determination of the issues.
b. Establish a commission, composed of representatives of the railroad carriers, railroad labor organizations, and public members, to survey the entire working rules problem and come forth with recommendations for changes. It would be most appropriate to make rules changes during a period of full employment so that the employment effects, if any, would be minimized.
c. The existing procedures for rate-determination and the entire question of competition in the field of transportation should be re-examined so that the railroad industry might be on a firmer financial footing.

These proposals are intended to achieve two objectives which are essential to the restoration of labor peace in the railroad industry: the restoration of genuine collective bargaining in the negotiation of new agreements and the elimination of the working-rules problem as a major source of conflict between the parties. The stumbling block, however, is whether or not both parties to the labor disputes will act in a responsible manner which, in the words of J. M. Clark "implies a range of inner discretion for the individual, which he exercises with a view to the rights of others; and . . . also implies some accountability to others for the use that is made of this discretion."[1] Failure of the leaders of both groups to accept this responsibility may (to paraphrase J. M. Clark) lead to no alternative but serfdom.

NOTES

I: INTRODUCTION

1. *Principles of Economics*, pp. 674–675.
2. Association of American Railroads, Bureau of Railway Economics, *Railroad Transportation, A Statistical Record, 1911–1949*, pp. 39–40.
3. Bonavia, *The Economics of Transport*, pp. 2–3.
4. In actual practice emergency boards have also been established for the purpose of hearing disputes arising out of the interpretation and application of collective bargaining agreements.
5. For a discussion of the other phases of industrial relations in the railroad industry see: Northrup, "Unfair Labor Practice Prevention Under the Railway Labor Act," *Industrial and Labor Relations Review*, III (April, 1950), 323–340; and by the same author, "The Appropriate Bargaining Unit Question Under the Railway Labor Act," *Quarterly Journal of Economics*, LX (February, 1946), 250–261.

II: RAILROAD INDUSTRY

1. Association of American Railroads, *A Review of Railway Operations in 1951*, p. 49; and *Railway Age*, January 12, 1953, p. 146.
2. Interstate Commerce Commission, *Wage Statistics of Class I Steam Railways in the United States*. Statement No. M-300, monthly reports for 1952 (hereafter referred to as I.C.C. Statement No. M-300).
3. For a map of railway lines in the United States see Locklin, *Economics of Transportation*, p. 124.
4. Interstate Commerce Commission, *Statistics of Railways in the United States*, 1950, p. 4.
5. *Ibid.*, p. 39.

6. *Ibid.*, pp. 306 ff.

7. United States District Court, Western District of New York, *United States of America v. Switchmen's Union of North America*, Civil No. 4638, August 11, 1950. Printed in *Journal of the Switchmen's Union of North America*, September, 1950, pp. 235 ff.

8. *Ibid.*

9. U.S. Congress, *To Prohibit Strikes and to Provide for Compulsory Arbitration in the Railroad Industry*, May 8 to July 3, 1950, p. 22. (Hereafter referred to as Hearings on the Donnell Resolution.)

10. Interstate Commerce Commission, *Factors in the Determination of Reasonable Levels of Fares for Motor Carriers of Passengers*, p. 1.

11. Carriers' Exhibit 38, *Financial Condition of the Railroads*, Presented to the Emergency Board appointed by the President on February 24, 1950, p. 18.

12. *Ibid.*, p. 3.

13. *Ibid.*, p. 6; and Interstate Commerce Commission, *Monthly Comment on Transportation Statistics*, August 13, 1948, p. 3.

14. Association of American Railroads, *A Review of Railway Operations in 1951*, p. 11; and *Railway Age*, January 12, 1953, p. 148.

15. Interstate Commerce Commission, *Factors in the Determination of Reasonable Levels of Fares for Motor Carriers of Passengers*, p. 41.

16. Dearing and Owen, *National Transportation Policy*, *passim*.

17. Carriers' Exhibit No. 38, *op. cit.*, Appendices 22 and 23.

18. Dearing and Owen, *op. cit.*, p. 270.

19. Williams, "An Evaluation of Public Policy Toward the Railway Industry," *American Economic Review, Papers and Proceedings*, XLI (May, 1951), 514–515.

20. *Ibid.*, p. 516.

21. Dearing and Owen, *op. cit.*, p. 273.

22. *Ibid.*, p. 278.

23. *Ibid.*, pp. 278–286.

24. Interstate Commerce Commission, *Monthly Comment on*

NOTES TO II: RAILROAD INDUSTRY

Transportation Statistics, February 15, 1950, p. 3; Dearing and Owen, *op. cit.*, pp. 285–286.

25. Dearing and Owen, *op. cit.*, p. 288.
26. Association of American Railroads, *A Review of Railway Operations in 1951*, p. 21; and *Railway Age*, January 12, 1953, p. 152.
27. U.S. Department of Labor, Bureau of Labor Statistics, *Monthly Labor Review*, January, 1953, p. 109.
28. *The Economic Report of the President*, Transmitted to the Congress January, 1953, p. 180.
29. Kaufman, "The Wage-Price Relationships in the Railroad Industry: A Comment," *Journal of Business*, XXVI (January, 1953), 48 ff.
30. Interstate Commerce Commission, *Monthly Comment on Transportation Statistics*, January 14, 1953, pp. 23.
31. *Ibid.*, April 1951, p. 3.
32. Kaufman, *loc. cit.*
33. Interstate Commerce Commission, *Monthly Comment on Transportation Statistics*, April 13, 1951, pp. 1–2.
34. *The New York Times*, August 9, 1951, and *Ex Parte* No. 175, August 8, 1951, and April 11, 1952. On March 27, 1953, the railroads petitioned to have the rate increase made permanent.
35. Dearing and Owen, *op.cit.*, p. 293.
36. *Ibid.*, Chapter XV.
37. Williams, "An Evaluation of Public Policy Toward the Railway Industry," *op. cit.*, p. 517.
38. Dearing and Owen, *op. cit.*, Chapter XV.
39. Twentieth Century Fund, Inc., *How Collective Bargaining Works*, p. 370. See also Baker, "The Possibilities of Economies by Railroad Consolidation and Coordination," *American Economic Review*, XXX (March, 1940), Part 2, Supplement, especially pp. 148–149.
40. 54 *U.S. Statutes at Large*, 76th Cong., 3rd Sess., Ch. 722, p. 906.
41. *Ibid.*
42. *Ibid.*
43. Twentieth Century Fund, Inc., *How Collective Bargaining Works*, p. 369.

44. *Ibid.*, pp. 369–370.
45. *Ibid.*
46. Kirkland, *Men, Cities, and Transportation*, II, 352–353.
47. Fabricant, *Labor Savings in American Industry 1899–1939*, pp. 46 ff.
48. I.C.C. Statement No. M-300, Years 1939 to 1950.
49. See Chapters III and XI.
50. Interstate Commerce Commission, *Statistics of Railways of Class I, United States*, 1948, p. 7; and *Railway Age*, January 12, 1953, p. 153.
51. Interstate Commerce Commission, *Yard Service Performance of Class I Steam Railways in the United States*, Statement No. M-215, December, 1950.
52. Interstate Commerce Commission, *Monthly Comment on Transportation Statistics*, July 13, 1951, p. 9.
53. *Ibid.*, July 13, 1950, pp. 7–8.
54. *Railway Age*, January 15, 1951, pp. 180 ff.
55. *Ibid.*
56. *Railway Age*, January 12, 1953, p. 152.

III: EMPLOYMENT

1. Fabricant, *Labor Savings in American Industry 1899–1939*, pp. 46, 50.
2. I.C.C. Statement No. M-300, Years 1939 and 1945.
3. I.C.C. Statement No. M-300, December, 1950.
4. I.C.C. Statement No. M-300, December, 1952.
5. Hultgren, *American Transportation in Prosperity and Depression*, p. 176.
6. Interstate Commerce Commission, *Statistics of Railways in the United States*, 1948, p. 155.
7. *Ibid.*
8. *Ibid.*
9. *Ibid.*, p. 39 and Interstate Commerce Commission, Statement No. M-300, 1945 and December, 1952; Interstate Commerce Commission, *Revenue Traffic Statistics of Class I Steam Railways in the United States*, Statement No. M-220, January through October, 1952; and *Railway Age*, January 12, 1953, p. 146.

NOTES TO III: EMPLOYMENT

10. *Ibid.*
11. Hultgren, *op. cit.*, chap. 14.
12. *Ibid.*, pp. 97–98.
13. See also Barger, *The Transportation Industries 1889–1946*, chap. iv.
14. I.C.C. Statement No. M-300, Year 1939 and December, 1950.
15. Interstate Commerce Commission, *Statistics of Railways*, 1948, p. 39; and *Railway Age*, January 12, 1953, p. 146.
16. I.C.C. Statement No. M-300, Year 1939 and Year 1950.
17. See Chapter VIII and IX where these issues are discussed in detail.
18. Monroe, *Railroad Men and Wages*, pp. 5, 37, and 38; and *Report to the President by the Emergency Board*, December 17, 1948, p. 37.
19. *Ibid.*, p. 5.
20. Federal Coordinator of Transportation, *A Survey of the Rules Governing the Wage Payments in Railroad Train and Engine Service*, I, 5.
21. *Ibid.*, pp. 1–3.
22. *Ibid.*, p. 6. An agreement, effective September 1, 1948 modified the "8 within 10" rule to an "8 within 9" rule. See *General Wage and Rule Agreements, Decisions, Awards and Orders, Governing Employees Engaged in Engine Service on Railroads in the United States, 1942–1948*, II, 99.
23. Monroe, *op. cit.*, p. 6.
24. *Ibid.*, p. 12.
25. Twentieth Century Fund, Inc., *How Collective Bargaining Works*, p. 349.
26. Federal Coordinator of Transportation, *op. cit.*, pp. 5–6.
27. Moulton, *The American Transportation Problem*, p. 190.
28. Kirkland, *Men, Cities, and Transportation*, II, 405–406.
29. *Report to the President by the Emergency Board*, April 18, 1946, p. 24.
30. Interstate Commerce Commission, *Statistics of Railways in the United States, 1948*, p. 16.
31. *Report to the President by the Emergency Board*, December 17, 1948, pp. 37–39.

32. *Report to the President by the Emergency Board*, June 15, 1950, pp. 167–168.

33. *Ibid.*, pp. 6–10.

34. Slichter, *Union Policies and Industrial Management*, p. 2.

35. *Transcript of Proceedings of the Emergency Board*, Chicago, Illinois, 1946, pp. 84 ff. (Hereafter referred to as the 1946 Transcript.)

36. *Ibid.*, p. 87.

37. See Chapter V for a discussion of these and other statutes.

38. 1946 Transcript, p. 88.

39. *Ibid.*

40. 39 *U.S. Statutes at Large*, 64th Cong., 1st Sess., Part I, Ch. 436, p. 721.

41. Reprinted in *General Wage and Rule Agreements, Decisions, Awards and Orders, Governing Employees Engaged in Engine Service on Railroads in the United States, 1907–1941*, I, 157–158.

42. *Ibid.*, pp. 158 ff.

43. *Ibid.*, p. 187.

44. 41 *U.S. Statutes at Large*, 66th Cong., 2nd Sess., Part I, Ch. 91, p. 456. See Title III.

45. 1946 Transcript, p. 92.

46. See Chapter XI for a discussion of the grievance procedure in the railroad industry.

47. 1946 Transcript, p. 85.

48. The description of the rules is based on *The Issues Before the Emergency Board and the Closing Argument for the Carriers in the Engineers' and Trainmen's Rules Case*, passim; and *General Wage and Rule Agreements, Decisions, Awards and Order*, Vols. I and II.

49. National Railroad Adjustment Board, First Division, Award No. 3110, XVII, 620. (Hereafter referred to as NRAB Awards, which are First Division awards unless otherwise noted.)

50. NRAB Award No. 5628, XXXII, 769.

51. NRAB Award No. 4363, XXVII, 236.

52. NRAB Award No. 3633, XXI, 77–81.

53. NRAB Award No. 8838, Vol. 57, 520–524.

54. *Ibid.*

55. *The Issues Before the Emergency Board and the Closing Argument for the Carriers in the Engineers' and Trainmen's Case*, p. 22.
56. NRAB Award No. 1716, IX, 39.
57. NRAB Award No. 4171, XXIV, 382–404.
58. *The Issues Before the Emergency Board and the Closing Argument for the Carriers in the Engineers' and Trainmen's Rules Case*, p. 138.
59. This rule was modified on the basis of an arbitration award which arose out of the 1952 settlement. See *Transcript of Proceedings of Emergency Board*, Chicago, Illinois, 1950, II, 2787 ff.
60. *Transcript of Proceedings of the Emergency Board*, Chicago, Illinois, 1948, Book 1, p. 1229. (Hereafter referred to as 1948 Transcript.)
61. *Report to the President by the Emergency Board*, October 29, 1938, p. 56.
62. 1948 Transcript, p. 1230.
63. *Supplementary Report to the President by the Emergency Board*, December 5, 1941, p. 12.
64. *Report to the President by the Emergency Board*, November 5, 1941, pp. 61 ff.
65. Agreement reprinted in *General Wage and Rule Agreements, Decisions, Awards and Orders*, II, 65 ff.
66. *Report to the President by the Emergency Board*, April 18, 1946, pp. 11–12.
67. Agreement reprinted in *General Wage and Rule Agreements, Decisions, Awards and Orders*, II, 85 ff.
68. *Report to the President by the Emergency Board*, March 27, 1948, *passim*.
69. *Ibid.*, pp. 56–57.
70. *Report to the President by the Emergency Board*, June 15, 1950, pp. 149–150. For a detailed description of this movement see *Seventeenth Annual Report of the National Mediation Board*, pp. 6 ff.
71. *Report to the President by the Emergency Board*, March 27, 1948, p. 46.
72. *Ibid.*, p. 53.
73. *Ibid.*, pp. 43–45, 55.

74. *Report to the President by the Emergency Board,* June 15, 1950, pp. 149–150.

75. *Ibid.,* p. 150.

76. *Seventeenth Annual Report of the National Mediation Board,* p. 12. In 1952, an emergency board recommended, in a case involving the firemen's organization, that these arbitrator's awards be accepted by the firemen and in addition recommended a revision of the switching limit and interdivisional run rules. See *Report to the President by the Emergency Board,* January 25, 1952.

77. *Seventeenth Annual Report of the National Mediation Board,* p. 25.

IV: LABOR ORGANIZATIONS

1. I.C.C. Statement No. M-300, December, 1952, and Hearings on the Donnell Resolution, p. 188.

2. *Eighteenth Annual Report of the National Mediation Board,* Table 12A (following p. 54).

3. Monroe, *Railroad Men and Wages,* pp. 2, 4.

4. I.C.C. Statement No. M-300, December, 1952.

5. Monroe, *op. cit.,* p. 4.

6. Peterson, *American Labor Unions,* Appendix D.

7. Harris, *American Labor,* p. 250.

8. Ross, *Trade Union Wage Policy,* p. 61.

9. *Ibid.*

10. See Harris, *op. cit.,* "The Railroad Unions."

11. Twentieth Century Fund, Inc., *How Collective Bargaining Works,* p. 324.

12. *Sixteenth Annual Report of the National Mediation Board,* p. 45.

13. Twentieth Century Fund, Inc., *op. cit.,* p. 325.

14. *Ibid.,* pp. 340, 369, 370, and 371.

15. 50 *U.S. Statutes at Large,* 75th Cong., 1st Sess., Part I, Ch. 382, p. 307.

16. Twentieth Century Fund, Inc., *op. cit.,* p. 341.

17. *Ibid.,* p. 342.

18. *Report to the President by the Emergency Board,* November 5, 1941, pp. 4 ff.

19. *Report to the President by the Emergency Board*, September 25, 1943.

20. *Report Covering the Wage Movement of 1943*, issued by the Brotherhood of Locomotive Firemen and Enginemen, Order of Railway Conductors, and the Switchmen's Union of North America, *passim* and pp. 7 ff., and 39 ff.

21. *Report to the President by the Emergency Board*, April 18, 1946.

22. *Report to the President by the Emergency Board*, June 15, 1950, p. 1.

23. *Report to the President by the Emergency Board*, April 18, 1950, p. 1.

24. *Ibid.*, pp. 7–8.

25. *The New York Times*, October 25, 1950.

26. Twentieth Century Fund, Inc., *op. cit.*, p. 352.

27. *Ibid.*, pp. 352–355.

28. *Brotherhood of Locomotive Firemen and Enginemen's Magazine*, December, 1949, p. 375.

29. *Eleventh Annual Report of the National Mediation Board*, p. 19.

30. Roe, *Juggernaut*, p. 267.

31. See, for example, the *Trainman News*, April 6, 1953, for a story on a decision of a special referee of a court who denied the United Railroad Operating Crafts' contention that it was "national in scope."

32. Peterson, *op. cit.*, Appendix D; Monroe, *op. cit.*, p. 2.

33. *The New York Times*, October 12, 1950.

V: FEDERAL INTERVENTION IN DISPUTES

1. 25 *United States Statutes at Large*, 50th Cong., 1st Sess., Ch. 1063, p. 501.

2. Yellen, *American Labor Struggles*, pp. 3 ff., 38.

3. Lindsey, *The Pullman Strike*, p. 8.

4. Fisher, *Use of Federal Power in Settlement of Railway Labor Disputes*, pp. 8–9.

5. Twentieth Century Fund, Inc., *Labor and the Government*, p. 173.

6. Fisher, *op. cit.*, p. 7.
7. *Ibid.*, p. 13.
8. *Ibid.*, pp. 14, 19. See also Commons and Andrews, *Principles of Labor Legislation*, pp. 138–139.
9. 30 *U.S. Statutes at Large*, 55th Cong., 2nd Sess., Ch. 370, p. 424.
10. See Lindsey, *op. cit.*, pp. 35 ff. for a discussion of the aftermath of the strike.
11. *Adair v. United States*, 208 U.S. 161 (1908).
12. Fisher, *op. cit.*, pp. 24–25.
13. *Ibid.*, pp. 31 and 62.
14. Commons and Andrews, *op. cit.*, p. 140. See also U.S. Department of Commerce and Labor, *Bulletin of the Bureau of Labor*, No. 98, January, 1912, "Mediation and Arbitration of Railway Labor Disputes in the United States," by Charles P. Neill, p. 2 and *passim*.
15. Fisher, *op. cit.*, pp. 34–35, and 38 ff.
16. *Ibid.*, pp. 45–48; and *Report of the Board of Arbitration in the Matter of Controversy Between the Eastern Railroads and the Brotherhood of Locomotive Engineers*, November 2, 1912. This report included (pp. 86 ff.) a recommendation for the compulsory arbitration of railroad labor disputes.
17. Fisher, *op. cit.*, pp. 44–45, and 54–55.
18. *Adair v. United States*, 208 U.S. 161 (1908).
19. Fisher, *op. cit.*, pp. 25–26.
20. 38 *U.S. Statutes at Large*, 63rd Cong., 1st Sess., Ch. 6, p. 103.
21. Fisher, *op. cit.*, p. 48.
22. *Ibid.*, p. 186.
23. Reprinted in *General Wage and Rule Agreements, Decisions, Awards and Orders, Governing Employees Engaged in Engine Service on Railroads in the United States, 1907–1941*, p. 75.
24. Fisher, *op. cit.*, pp. 52 ff.
25. *Ibid.*, pp. 59–60.
26. 39 *U.S. Statutes at Large*, 64th Cong., 1st Sess., Part I, Ch. 436, p. 721.
27. Commons and Andrews, *op. cit.*, p. 143.

NOTES TO V: FEDERAL INTERVENTION IN DISPUTES 197

28. 39 *U.S. Statutes at Large*, 64th Cong., 1st Sess., Part I, Ch. 436, p. 721.

29. Fisher, *op. cit.*, p. 60.

30. The mediation award is reprinted in *General Wage and Rule Agreements, Decisions, Awards and Orders, Governing Employees Engaged in Engine Service on Railroads in the United States, 1907–1941*, p. 157.

31. *Wilson v. New*, 243 U.S. 332 (1917).

32. Fisher, *op. cit.*, pp. 67–68.

33. *First Annual Report of the National Mediation Board*, p. 62.

34. *Ibid.*, p. 63.

35. Fisher, *op. cit.*, p. 75.

36. Twentieth Century Fund, Inc., *How Collective Bargaining Works*, p. 327.

37. 41 *U.S. Statutes at Large*, 66th Cong., 2nd Sess., Part I, Ch. 91, p. 456. See Title III.

38. Fisher, *op. cit.*, pp. 76–85.

39. Witte, *The Government in Labor Disputes*, p. 241.

40. *First Annual Report of the National Mediation Board*, p. 63.

41. Witte, *op. cit.*, p. 241, and Fisher, *op. cit.*, p. 96.

42. Twentieth Century Fund, Inc., *How Collective Bargaining Works*, p. 327.

43. For the definitive work on the Railroad Labor Board see Wolf, *The Railroad Labor Board*.

44. Twentieth Century Fund, Inc., *Labor and the Government*, p. 183.

45. *Ibid.*, p. 181.

46. Witte, *op. cit.*, pp. 241–242.

47. Twentieth Century Fund, Inc., *How Collective Bargaining Works*, pp. 328–329.

48. Wolf, *op. cit.*, p. 365.

49. Twentieth Century Fund, Inc., *Labor and the Government*, p. 182.

50. Wolf, *op. cit.*, p. 371.

51. *Pennsylvania Railroad Co. v. U.S. Railroad Labor Board et al.*, 261 U.S. 72 (1922).

52. Wolf, *op. cit.*, p. 384.
53. *First Annual Report of the National Mediation Board*, p. 64.
54. 44 *U.S. Statutes at Large*, 69th Cong., 1st Sess., Part 2, Ch. 347, p. 579.
55. Fisher, "The New Railway Labor Act: A Comparison and Appraisal," *American Economic Review*, XVII (March, 1927), 187.
56. Witte, *op. cit.*, pp. 242–243.
57. Ellingwood, "The Railway Labor Act of 1926," *Journal of Political Economy*, XXXVI (February, 1928), 63.
58. Witte, *op. cit.*, p. 244.
59. Fisher, "The New Railway Labor Act: A Comparison and Appraisal," *op. cit.*, pp. 185–186.
60. Witte, *op. cit.*, p. 244.
61. Moulton, *The American Transportation Problem*, p. 197.
62. Twentieth Century Fund, Inc., *Labor and the Government*, pp. 184–189.
63. Monroe, *op. cit.*, p. 40.
64. *The Economic Report of the President*, January, 1953, p. 180.
65. *First Annual Report of the National Mediation Board*, p. 65.
66. 47 *U.S. Statutes at Large*, 72nd Cong., 2nd Sess., Ch. 204, p. 1467.
67. 48 *U.S. Statutes at Large*, 73rd Cong., 1st Sess., Ch. 91, p. 211.
68. *Texas and New Orleans Railroad Company et al. v. Brotherhood of Railway and Steamship Clerks et al.*, 281 U.S. 548 (1930).
69. 48 *U.S. Statutes at Large*, 73rd Cong., 2nd Sess., Ch. 691, p. 1185.
70. See Chapter XI for a description and analysis of the Board's activities.
71. The law was amended in 1951 to allow for the union shop and the check-off of union dues (Public Law 914, Ch. 1220, 81st Cong., 2nd Sess.).
72. Twentieth Century Fund, Inc., *How Collective Bargaining Works*, pp. 359, 374–375.

73. Kaltenborn, *Governmental Adjustment of Labor Disputes*, p. 72.

74. Northrup, "The Railway Labor Act and Railroad Labor Disputes in Wartime," *American Economic Review*, XXXVI (June, 1946), 324.

75. *First Annual Report of the National Mediation Board*, p. 1.

76. *Sixteenth Annual Report of the National Mediation Board*, p. 6.

77. See Chapter VII.

78. *Sixteenth Annual Report of the National Mediation Board*, pp. 7, 23–26, and 33.

79. U.S. Cong., Senate. *Dispute Between the Railway Carriers and Four Operating Brotherhoods*, June 27, 1951, *passim*.

80. See Chapter XIV.

VI: THE ACT

1. Quoted in Kaltenborn, *Governmental Adjustment of Labor Disputes*, p. 72.

2. *The New York Times*, March 8, 1951.

3. Twentieth Century Fund, Inc., *How Collective Bargaining Works*, p. 373. In 1946, a similar appraisal was made by another student of railroad labor: see Otto S. Beyer, "The Railway Labor Act," *Proceedings of the Academy of Political Science*, XXII (1946–1948), 51.

4. Bloom and Northrup, *Economics of Labor and Industrial Relations*, p. 627.

5. Northrup, "Emergency Disputes Under the Railway Labor Act," *Proceedings of First Annual Meeting*, Industrial Relations Research Association, 1948, pp. 79, 87.

6. *Sixth Annual Report of the National Mediation Board*, p. 1.

7. *Sixteenth Annual Report of the National Mediation Board*, p. 3.

8. *Ibid.*, p. 7, and *passim*.

VII: THE RECORD

1. *Sixteenth Annual Report of the National Mediation Board*, pp. 6, 33; and Kaltenborn, *Governmental Adjustment of Labor Disputes*, pp. 65–66.

2. *Eighteenth Annual Report of the National Mediation Board,* p. 3.

3. *Ibid.*

4. Bloom and Northrup, *Economics of Labor and Industrial Relations,* p. 627.

5. Monroe, *Railroad Men and Wages,* p. 40.

6. *The Economic Report of the President,* January, 1953, p. 180.

7. *Sixteenth Annual Report of the National Mediation Board,* p. 6.

8. See Kaltenborn, *op. cit.,* pp. 224–230.

9. *Tenth Annual Report of the National Mediation Board,* pp. 1–2.

10. *Sixteenth Annual Report of the National Mediation Board,* p. 3.

11. Twentieth Century Fund, Inc., *How Collective Bargaining Works,* pp. 374–375.

12. U.S. Department of Labor, *Monthly Labor Review,* January, 1951, "Analysis of Strikes, 1927–1949."

13. Hearings on the Donnell Resolution, pp. 196–201.

14. *Eighteenth Annual Report of the National Mediation Board,* pp. 20–21.

15. *Sixteenth Annual Report of the National Mediation Board,* p. 52.

16. Bloom and Northrup, *op. cit.,* p. 624.

17. *Sixteenth Annual Report of the National Mediation Board,* p. 52.

18. Bloom and Northrup, *op. cit.,* p. 624.

19. Monroe, *op. cit.,* pp. 40–41.

20. *Report of the Emergency Board to the President,* October 29, 1938, p. 56.

21. Monroe, *op. cit.,* pp. 41–42.

22. *Supplementary Report to the President by the Emergency Board, Mediation Settlement,* December 5, 1941, p. 6.

23. *Ibid.,* p. 7.

24. Monroe, *op. cit.,* p. 43.

25. Northrup, "The Railway Labor Act and Railway Labor

NOTES TO VII: THE RECORD

Disputes in Wartime," *American Economic Review*, XXXVI (June 1946), 330.

26. Monroe, *op. cit.*, p. 44.

27. *Ibid.*

28. Northrup, *op. cit.*, pp. 330–331, 333.

29. Boards of Arbitration, National Mediation Board, Docket No. A-2215, Arb. 61 and 62, and *Report to the President by the Emergency Board*, April 18, 1946.

30. Monroe, *op. cit.*, pp. 47–48.

31. Northrup, *op. cit.*, pp. 342–343, n. 37.

32. *Employees' National Conference Committee and Eastern, Western and Southeastern Carriers' Conference Committee*, Board of Arbitration, NMB Case A-2595, Arbitration 91, Award, September 2, 1947.

33. U.S. Department of Labor, *Monthly Labor Review*, June, 1948, p. 645; and *Report to the President by the Emergency Board*, March 27, 1948.

34. *United States v. Brotherhood of Locomotives Engineers et al.*, 79 Federal Supplement 485 (1948).

35. U.S. Department of Labor, *Monthly Labor Review*, August, 1948, p. 152.

36. Bloom and Northrup, *op. cit.*, p. 624.

37. *Report to the President by the Emergency Board*, December 17, 1948, pp. 37–39.

38. *Sixteenth Annual Report of the National Mediation Board*, pp. 11–13.

39. *Ibid.*, p. 13, n. 1; see *Journal of Switchmen's Union of North America*, September, 1950, pp. 235 ff., for decision of court.

40. *The New York Times*, August 27, 1950.

41. *Ibid.*, December 15 and December 22, 1950.

42. *Ibid.*, January 7 and 8, 1951.

43. *United States v. Brotherhood of Railroad Trainmen et al.*, 95 Federal Supplement 101 (1951).

44. *The New York Times*, March 2, 1950.

45. *Ibid.*, May 26, 1951.

46. *Eighteenth Annual Report of the National Mediation Board*, p. 8.

VIII: EARNINGS POSITION OF WORKERS

1. Ross, *Trade Union Wage Policy*, p. 61.
2. See *Referee's Memorandum and Award*, March 18, 1953. involving the question of whether a wage increase based on changes in productivity is justified.
3. *Ibid.*
4. The Consumer Price Index (old series) increased 93 percent during this period. See U.S. Department of Labor, *Monthly Labor Review*, March 1953, p. 345.
5. See p. 113.
6. I.C.C. Statement No. M-300, Year 1936 and December, 1952.

IX: WAGE STANDARDS

1. The sole exception was the rejection of an emergency board's recommendations on the union shop for nonoperating worker's in 1952.
2. Metz, *Labor Policy of the Federal Government*, p. 205.
3. Dunlop, "The Economics of Wage-Dispute Settlement," *Law and Contemporary Problems, Labor Dispute Settlement*, XII (Spring, 1947), 293–294.
4. Dale, *Source of Economic Information for Collective Bargaining, passim.*
5. See Slichter, *The Challenge of Industrial Relations*, pp. 168–170.
6. Slichter, *Basic Criteria Used in Wage Negotiations*, pp. 8–9.
7. For a technical description of the index and its limitations see U.S. Department of Labor, Bureau of Labor Statistics, Bulletin No. 993, *Techniques of Preparing Major BLS Statistical Series*, 1950, pp. 1–6.
8. Office of Economic Stabilization, *Report of the President's Committee on the Cost of Living, 1945, passim.*
9. *Report of the Emergency Board to the President*, October 29, 1938.
10. *Ibid.*, pp. 8–19, 20.
11. *Ibid.*, p. 23.
12. *Ibid.*, p. 33.

NOTES TO IX: WAGE STANDARDS

13. *Ibid.*, pp. 25–37, 39, 41–56.
14. *Ibid.*, pp. 21, 31.
15. *Report to the President by the Emergency Board*, November 5, 1941.
16. *Ibid.*, pp. 12–17, 19–20, and 40.
17. *Ibid.*, pp. 40–47.
18. *Ibid.*, pp. 22–56, and Appendix E.
19. *Ibid.*, pp. 41, 43–44.
20. *Supplementary Report to the President by the Emergency Board*, December 5, 1941, p. 10.
21. *Ibid.*, p. 13.
22. *Report to the President by the Emergency Board*, May 24, 1943.
23. *Supplemental Report to the President by the Emergency Board*, May 29, 1943.
24. *Ibid.*, p. 95.
25. 1 War Labor Reports 325.
26. 9 War Labor Reports, xii–xv.
27. *Report to the President by the Emergency Board*, September 25, 1943, p. 84.
28. Monroe, *Railroad Men and Wages*, pp. 44–45.
29. *Report to the President by the Emergency Board*, April 18, 1946.
30. *Ibid.*; and Boards of Arbitration, National Mediation Board, Docket No. A-2215, Arb. 61 and 62.
31. *Ibid.*, pp. 8–9.
32. National Mediation Board, Docket No. A-2215, Arb. 62, Separate Opinion . . . , p. 13.
33. Board of Arbitration, NMB Case A-2595, Arbitration 91, Award, September 2, 1947.
34. *Report to the President by the Emergency Board*, March 27, 1948, p. 6.
35. *Ibid.*
36. *General Wage and Rule Agreements, Decisions, Awards and Orders, Governing Employees Engaged in Engine Service on Railroads in the United States, op. cit.*, p. 113.
37. *Report to the President by the Emergency Board*, December 17, 1948, p. 27.
38. *Ibid.*, pp. 29–34.

39. *Report to the President by the Emergency Board*, June 15, 1950.
40. *Ibid.*, pp. 45–46.
41. *Ibid.*, pp. 26–45.
42. U.S. Department of Labor, Bureau of Labor Statistics, *Cost of Living Wage Adjustments in Collective Bargaining*, September, 1950, pp. 15–16.
43. *The New York Times*, March 2, 1951.
44. *Report to the President by the Emergency Board*, September 25, 1943, p. 41.
45. See Table 3, Chapter VIII.
46. "Cost of Living Wage Clauses and the UAW-GM Pact," *Monthly Labor Review*, July, 1948, p. 5.
47. Ross, "The General Motors Wage Agreement of 1948," *Review of Economics and Statistics*, XXXI (February, 1949), 2, 4.
48. See Slichter, *Basic Criteria Used in Wage Negotiations*, p. 290; Ross, *op. cit.*, p. 3; and Reder, "The Significance of the 1948 General Motors Agreement," *Review of Economics and Statistics*, XXXI (February, 1949), 3–9.
49. Slichter, *Basic Criteria Used in Wage Negotiations*, p. 33.
50. *Ibid.*, p. 34.
51. *Ibid.*
52. *General Regulation* No. 8, issued by the Economic Stabilization Administrator, March 8, 1951, revised August 23, 1951, and amended effective December 7, 1951.
53. Ross, "The General Motors Wage Agreement of 1948," *op. cit.*, p. 5.
54. See, for example, Slichter, *Basic Criteria Used in Wage Negotiations*, p. 21; Hansen, "Stability and Expansion," in *Financing American Prosperity*, pp. 257–260; and Slichter, *The Challenge of Industrial Relations*, pp. 88–89.
55. *Transcript of Proceedings of the Emergency Board*, Chicago, Illinois, 1948, pp. 434–435.
56. See, for example, Carriers Exhibit No. 37, *Productivity of the Railroad Industry*, presented to the Emergency Board, Appointed by the President on February 24, 1950.
57. *Report of the Emergency Board to the President*, October 29, 1938, pp. 41–42.

NOTES TO IX: WAGE STANDARDS 205

58. *Report to the President by the Emergency Board*, November 5, 1941, p. 25.
59. *Report to the President by the Emergency Board*, September 25, 1943, pp. 45–46.
60. *Ibid.*, pp. 37–42.
61. *Report to the President by the Emergency Board*, December 17, 1948, p. 17.
62. *Report to the President by the Emergency Board*, June 15, 1950, pp. 28–29.
63. Eastern Railroad Presidents Conference, *Railroad Data*, March 27, 1953.
64. U.S. Department of Labor, Bureau of Labor Statistics, Bulletin No. 993, *Techniques of Preparing Major BLS Statistical Series*, 1950, pp. 42–49; and Fabricant, "Of Productivity Statistics: An Admonition," *Review of Economics and Statistics*, XXXI (November, 1949), 309–311.
65. Kerr, "The Short-Run Behavior of Physical Productivity and Average Hourly Earnings," *Review of Economics and Statistics*, XXXI (November, 1949), 299.
66. In 1936 and December, 1952 average hourly earnings of workers in manufacturing industries were 55.6 cents and 173.2 cents respectively, compared with 65.9 cents and 189.9 cents for railroad workers. During this period the index of consumer prices (old series) rose from 99.1 to 191.3 (1935–1939 = 100). See *The Economic Report of the President*, January, 1953, pp. 180, 190; and U.S. Department of Labor, Bureau of Labor Statistics, *Hours and Earnings*, February, 1953, p. 3.
67. I.C.C. Statement No. M-300, 1936, and December, 1952; see also footnote 66 above.
68. Estimates for manufacturing industries based on data of Kerr, *op. cit.*, p. 301, for 1936 to 1948. It is assumed that the average increase in output per man-hour for these years—2 percent—continued from 1949 and 1952. The output per man-hour for the railroad industry is estimated on the basis of traffic units (a weight combination of passenger-miles and revenue ton-miles) and man-hours paid for. See Association of American Railways, *Railroad Transportation, A Statistical Record*, 1911–1949, for data for years 1936 to 1949; *Railway Age*, January 12, 1953, p. 146; and Inter-

state Commerce Commission, Statement No. 300, for the years 1950 to 1952.

69. Slichter, *Basic Criteria Used in Wage Negotiations*, pp. 22–24.

70. Mills, *Prices in Recession and Recovery*, pp. 430–466; Hansen, "Stability and Expansion," Ellis, "Economic Expansion Through Competitive Markets," *Financing American Prosperity*, pp. 183–184.

71. Clark, *Alternative to Serfdom*, p. 132. See also Hansen, "Perspectives on Wage-Price Problems," in *Wages, Prices, and the National Welfare*, p. 3.

72. *Report to the President of the United States on the Labor Dispute in the Basic Steel Industry*, September 10, 1949, p. 45; for a summary of report see 3 American Labor Arbitration Awards 68, 318.

73. On June 6, 1951, the Wage Stabilization Board permitted a wage increase for certain automobile workers on the basis of productivity changes. This increase was in addition to that permitted on the basis of a change in the cost of living. See *The New York Times*, June 7, 1951.

74. See Meyers, "Criteria in the Making of Wage Decisions by 'Neutrals': The Railroads as a Case Study," *Industrial and Labor Relations Review*, 4 (April, 1951), 343; Kaufman, "Wage Criteria in the Railroad Industry," *Industrial and Labor Relations Review*, 6 (October, 1952), 119.

75. *Report of the Emergency Board to the President*, October 29, 1938, p. 50.

76. *Ibid.*, pp. 21–22, 35–37.

77. *Ibid.*, pp. 42–44.

78. *Report to the President of the Emergency Board*, November 5, 1941, pp. 27–46.

79. *Supplemental Report to the President by the Emergency Board*, May 29, 1943, pp. 95–96.

80. *Report to the President by the Emergency Board*, September 25, 1943, pp. 42, 84.

81. Executive Order 9697, *Federal Register*, Vol. 11, No. 34, p. 1691, and Order of the Economic Stabilization Director, *Federal Register*, Vol. 11, No. 29, p. 2517.

NOTES TO IX: WAGE STANDARDS

82. National Mediation Board, Docket No. A-2215, Arb. 62, Special Opinion . . . , p. 5.

83. *Report to the President by the Emergency Board*, April 18, 1946, pp. 8–9.

84. Board of Arbitration, NMB Case A-2591, Arbitration Award, and *Report to the President by the Emergency Board*, March 27, 1948, p. 6.

85. U.S. Department of Labor, *Monthly Labor Review*, July, 1947, p. 2.

86. *Report to the President by the Emergency Board*, March 27, 1948, p. 6.

87. *Report to the President by the Emergency Board*, December 17, 1948, p. 30.

88. *Ibid.*, p. 14.

89. *Report to the President by the Emergency Board*, June 15, 1950, pp. 8–9.

90. *Ibid.*, pp. 34–35.

91. *Ibid.*, pp. 8–9, 43–46.

92. See, for example, Dunlop, *op. cit.*, pp. 282–286; and Slichter, *Basic Criteria Used in Wage Negotiations*, pp. 36–40.

93. *Report to the President by the Emergency Board*, June 15, 1950.

94. *Ibid.*, and *Report to the President by the Emergency Board*, December 17, 1948, pp. 13–14.

95. *Report to the President by the Emergency Board*, December 17, 1948, pp. 37–38.

96. *Ibid.*, pp. 11–14.

97. *Report to the President by the Emergency Board*, June 15, 1950, p. 26.

98. *Ibid.*, pp. 26–45.

99. See Bloom and Northrup, *Economics of Labor and Industrial Relations*, pp. 524–525; and Northrup and Brinberg, *Economics of the Work Week*.

100. See Chapter II.

101. Locklin, *Economics of Transportation*, p. 342.

102. See Carriers Exhibit 38, *Financial Condition of the Railroads*, Presented to the Emergency Board Appointed by the President on February 24, 1950, *passim*.

103. 54 *U.S. Statutes at Large*, 76th Cong., 3rd Sess., Part I, Ch. 722, p. 898, Title 1, Section I.
104. *Report of the Emergency Board to the President*, October 29, 1938, pp. 25, 27.
105. *Ibid.*, pp. 26–27.
106. *Report to the President by the Emergency Board*, November 5, 1941, pp. 13–14 and similar report, dated May 29, 1943, pp. 45–47.
107. *Report of the Emergency Board to the President*, October 29, 1938, pp. 28, and 54.
108. *Report to the President by the Emergency Board*, November 5, 1941, pp. 52–56.
109. *Supplemental Report to the President by the Emergency Board*, May 29, 1943, pp. 68–69.
110. *Report to the President by the Emergency Board*, September 25, 1943, p. 60.
111. *Report to the President by the Emergency Board*, April 18, 1946, p. 8.
112. *Report to the President by the Emergency Board*, December 17, 1948, pp. 15–22, and 30.
113. *Report to the President by the Emergency Board*, June 15, 1950, pp. 31, and 166–167.
114. *Supplemental Report to the President by the Emergency Board*, May 29, 1943, pp. 64–69.
115. See Taylor, "Can Wages Be Left to Collective Bargaining," *Wages, Prices, and the National Welfare*, p. 32.
116. *Ibid.*, pp. 34–36. See also Dunlop, "Fact-Finding in Labor Disputes," *Proceedings of the Academy of Political Science*, XXII (1946–1948), 68.

X: SETTLEMENT OF DISPUTES

1. Hearings on the Donnell Resolution, p. 151.
2. *Fourteenth Annual Report of the National Mediation Board*, p. 4.
3. 39 *U.S. Statutes at Large*, 64th Cong., 1st Sess., Part I, Ch. 48, p. 643.
4. Brief for appellee, United States of America, U.S. Court of

Appeals, District of Columbia, *Brotherhood of Locomotive Engineers, et al. v. United States of America*, p. 16.

5. *Ibid.*, pp. 28–30.
6. *Ibid.*, pp. 30–31.
7. *United States v. Brotherhood of Locomotive Engineers et al.*, 79 Federal Supplement 485 (1948).
8. Brief for appellee, *op. cit.*, p. 16.
9. *United States v. Brotherhood of Locomotive Engineers et al.*, 79 Federal Supplement 485 (1948).
10. U.S. Cong., Senate, *Labor Relations*, Part I, pp. 277–278.
11. *Ibid.*, pp. 261 and 263.
12. *United States v. Brotherhood of Locomotive Engineers et al.*, 79 Federal Supplement at 488.
13. The Supreme Court denied a writ of certiorari in this case; see 69 Supreme Court 137 (1948).
14. See *Journal of Switchmen's Union of North America*, September, 1950, pp. 235 ff. for the decision of the Court.
15. *Youngstown Sheet and Tube Co., et al. v. Charles Sawyer*, decided June 2, 1952.
16. See Berman, *Labor Disputes and the President*.
17. Slichter, "The Great Question in Industrial Relations," *New York Times Magazine*, April 27, 1947, pp. 5 ff.
18. Roe, *Juggernaut*, p. 285.
19. *Ibid.*, pp. 293–294.
20. *Ibid.*, pp. 296–297. See also Whitney, *Railroad Rules and Wages Movement in United States 1944–45–46*.
21. *The New York Times*, January 5, 1951.
22. *The New York Times*, December 28, 1950.
23. U.S. Cong., Senate, *Labor Dispute Between Railroad Carriers and Four Operating Brotherhoods*, February 22 to April 5, 1951, pp. 42–43. (Hereafter referred to as Hearings on Railroad Labor Dispute, 1951.)
24. *Ibid.*, p. 132.
25. *Ibid.*, pp. 503 ff.

XI: GRIEVANCE PROCEDURES

1. This chapter was published in the *Southern Economic Journal*, July, 1952. Only minor changes have been made here.

2. Slichter, *Union Policies and Industrial Management*, p. 1.
3. *Ibid.*
4. 48 *U.S. Statutes at Large* 211, Ch. 91, 73rd Cong., 1st Sess.
5. Chamberlain, *Collective Bargaining*, p. 99.
6. *Ibid.*
7. *Ibid.*, pp. 113 ff.
8. Spencer, *The National Railroad Adjustment Board*, pp. 11–12.
9. *Ibid.*, p. 12.
10. National Railroad Adjustment Board, *Organization and Certain Rules of Procedure*, Circular No. 1 issued October 10, 1934; Reprinted February 1, 1939: Chicago, Illinois.
11. For a full discussion of procedures see Spencer, *op. cit.*; and Garrison, "The National Railroad Adjustment Board: A Unique Administrative Agency," *Yale Law Journal*, XLVI (February, 1937), 567.
12. Spencer, *op. cit.*, p. 17.
13. Jones, (ed.), *Inquiry of the Attorney-General's Committee on Administrative Procedure and Historical Background and Growth of Machinery Set Up for the Handling of Railroad Labor Disputes 1888–1940*, Bk. I, p. 212.
14. *Ibid.*, Bk. I, p. 221.
15. *Ibid.*, Bk. I, p. 279.
16. This procedure was primarily designed to handle disputes arising out of changes in the collective bargaining agreements, but in actual practice emergency boards have heard grievance disputes.
17. *Ibid.*, pp. 60–63; see *Report to the President by the Emergency Board*, April 29, 1949, particularly pp. 2–4.
18. Jones, *op. cit.*, p. 25.
19. *Ibid.*, p. 63.
20. Hearings on the Donnell Resolution, pp. 289–290.
21. Loomis, *Railway Labor Legislation*, p. 33.
22. Jones, *op. cit.*, Book I, pp. 275–276; and Loomis, *op. cit.*, pp. 27 ff.
23. *Sixteenth Annual Report of the National Mediation Board*, p. 24.

24. *Eighteenth Annual Report of the National Mediation Board*, p. 58.
25. *Ibid.*
26. *Ibid.* p. 76.
27. *Sixteenth Annual Report of the National Mediation Board*, p. 24.
28. *Eighteenth Annual Report of the National Mediation Board*, p. 58. It has been noted that the labor organizations may bring cases before the Board which have little merit so as to avoid a large proportion of cases being decided in favor of labor. See Jones, *op. cit.*, Book I, p. 109, n. 47.
29. Jones, *op. cit.*, Book I, pp. 86 ff.
30. *Eighteenth Annual Report of the National Mediation Board*, p. 3.
31. Loomis, *op. cit.*, pp. 27–29.
32. Cottrell, "Death by Dieselization: A Case Study in the Reaction to Technological Change," *American Sociological Review*, XVI (June, 1951), 358.
33. Jones, *op. cit.*, Book I, p. 300.
34. *Ibid.*, p. 288.
35. Hearings on the Donnell Resolution, pp. 289 ff. and 163 ff.
36. *Sixteenth Annual Report of the National Mediation Board*, pp. 24–25.
37. Hearings on the Donnell Resolution, p. 289.
38. Jones, *op. cit.*, Book I, pp. 238–239.
39. Hearings on the Donnell Resolution, p. 289.
40. Slichter, *Union Policies and Industrial Management*, pp. 195–196, especially n. 80.
41. Hearings on the Donnell Resolution, p. 90.
42. *Ibid.*, pp. 289–290.
43. *Ibid.*
44. Jones, *op. cit.*, Book I, p. 275.
45. Hearings on the Donnell Resolution, p. 164.
46. Jones, *op. cit.*, Book I, p. 245.
47. Hearings on the Donnell Resolution, p. 90.
48. *Ibid.*, p. 113; and *Sixteenth Annual Report of the National Mediation Board*, p. 76.
49. Garrison, "Labor Relations in the Railroad Industry,"

Proceedings of the Academy of Political Science, XVII (1936–1938), 169.

50. Hearings on Railroad Labor Dispute, 1951, *passim*.

51. Referee's Decision and Award, *In the Matter of a Controversy Between Brotherhood of Railroad Trainmen and Certain Participating Eastern, Western, and Southeastern Railroads of the United States*, August 1, 1951.

52. Letter, General Chairman of Grievance Committee, Brotherhood of Locomotive Firemen and Enginemen, New York Central Lines West, August 7, 1951.

53. Garrison, "The National Railroad Adjustment Board . . . ," *op. cit.*, p. 590.

54. *Ibid., passim*.

55. "Railroad Labor Disputes and the National Railroad Adjustment Board," *The University of Chicago Review*, XVIII, Winter, 1951, 303. The cases referred to are *Slocum v. Delaware, Lackawanna, and Western Railroad Co.*, 339 U.S. 239 (1950) and *Order of Railway Conductors v. Southern Railway Co.*, 339 U.S. 255 (1950).

56. *Ibid., passim*.

57. Williams, "An Evaluation of Public Policy Toward the Railway Industry," *American Economic Review, Papers and Proceedings*, pp. 517–518.

XII: DEFECTS IN THE ACT

1. Hearings on the Donnell Resolution, pp. 8, 14, 32, 34, 42.
2. *Ibid.*, pp. 15–16, and *passim*.
3. *Ibid.*, pp. 179–180.
4. Slichter, "The Great Question in Industrial Relations" *The New York Times Magazine*, April 27, 1947; Bloom and Northrup, *Economics of Labor and Industrial Relations*, pp. 628–630; Dunlop, "Fact-Finding in Labor Disputes," *Proceedings of the Academy of Political Science*, p. 73.
5. Hearings on the Donnell Resolution, pp. 15–16.
6. *Ibid.*, p. 16.
7. See U.S. Department of Labor, *The Termination Report, National War Labor Board*, I, 532–533; and Taylor, *Government Regulation of Industrial Relations*, chaps. 3 and 4.

NOTES TO XII: DEFECTS IN THE ACT 213

8. *Ibid.*
9. Bloom and Northrup, *op. cit.*, p. 647.
10. Hearings on the Donnell Resolution, pp. 179–180.
11. *Ibid.*, p. 180.
12. *Ibid.*, p. 181. This argument is also made by Kennedy, "The Handling of Emergency Disputes," Industrial Relations Research Association, *Proceedings of Second Annual Meeting*, 1949, p. 23.
13. Stewart and Couper, *Fact-Finding in Industrial Disputes*, *passim*.
14. Slichter, "The Great Question in Industrial Relations," *op. cit.*, p. 5.
15. U.S. Department of Labor, Bureau of Labor Statistics, *Federal Fact-Finding Boards and Boards of Inquiry*, *passim*.
16. U.S. Department of Labor, *Report and Recommendations of the Fact-Finding Board . . . in the Dispute Between the Milwaukee Gas Light Co. and Local 18, United Gas, Coke, and Chemical Workers of America (CIO)*, September 1, 1946.
17. *Eighteenth Annual Report of the National Mediation Board*, p. 24.
18. *Railway Age*, March 16, 1953, pp. 12–14.
19. *Sixteenth Annual Report of the National Mediation Board*, pp. 7, 33 ff.
20. *Fourteenth Annual Report of the National Mediation Board*, p. 2.
21. Hearings on the Donnell Resolution, pp. 344–345.
22. *Report to the President by the Emergency Board*, June 15, 1950, p. 1.
23. *Report to the President by the Emergency Board*, March 27, 1948, pp. 1–2.
24. Monroe, *Railroad Men and Wages*, pp. 46–48.
25. *Ibid.*, pp. 43–45.
26. *Sixteenth Annual Report of the National Mediation Board*, p. 33.
27. *Report to the President by the Emergency Board*, March 27, 1948, p. 6. In 1951, the Wage Stabilization Board approved wage increases, for trainmen, which were in excess of the 10 percent formula, "in the light of the lengthy and complex negotia-

tion procedures provided by law for the railroad industry." See *The New York Times*, June 13, 1951.

28. *Sixteenth Annual Report of the National Mediation Board*, p. 34.

29. *Ibid.*

30. *Ibid.*

31. *Report to the President by the Emergency Board*, March 27, 1948, pp. 56–57.

XIII: THE RIGHT TO STRIKE

1. Edwin E. Witte, *op. cit.*, p. 18. See *Clements et al. v. United States*, 297 Federal Reporter 206, and 266 U.S. 605 (1924).

2. Section 2.

3. Quoted in U.S. Cong., Senate, *Labor Relations*, Part 6, p. 3020.

4. Hearings on the Donnell Resolution, p. 387.

5. *Ibid.*, pp. 387–388.

6. *Dorchy v. Kansas*, 272 U.S. 306, and at 311 (1926).

7. *United Auto Workers v. Wisconsin Employment Relations Board*, 336 U.S. 245, at 260 (1949).

8. Taylor, "Is Compulsory Arbitration Inevitable?," Industrial Relations Research Association, *Proceedings of First Annual Meeting*, 1948, p. 66.

9. *Ibid.*, pp. 75–76.

10. See Chapter XII.

11. Taylor, "Is Compulsory Arbitration Inevitable?," *op. cit.*, p. 67.

12. U.S. Department of Labor, *Monthly Labor Review*, "Settlement of Industrial Disputes in Seven Foreign Countries," August, 1946, p. 6.

13. Millis and Montgomery, *Organized Labor*, pp. 803, 821–822.

14. Kansas Laws, Special Session, 1920, c. 29.

15. *Wolff Packing Company v. Court of Industrial Relations*, 262 U.S. 522 (1923) and 267 U.S. 552 (1925).

16. Roberts, "Compulsory Arbitration of Labor Disputes in Public Utilities," *Labor Law Journal*, I (June, 1950), 702.

17. *Ibid.*, p. 696.

18. Kennedy, "*The Handling of Emergency Disputes*," *op. cit.*, p. 27.
19. *Ibid.*, p. 20. See also MacDonald, "Compulsory Arbitration in New Jersey," *Second Annual Conference on Labor*, Appendix C.
20. France and Lester, *Compulsory Arbitration of Utility Disputes in New Jersey and Pennsylvania*, pp. 43, 44, and 80–81.
21. See, for example, Shishkin, "The Case Against Compulsory Arbitration," *American Federationist*, February, 1947; U.S. Cong., Senate, *Labor Relations*, Part 2, pp. 828–829; U.S. Cong., Senate, *Labor Relations Program*, Part II (1947), p. 953.
22. Hearings on the Donnell Resolution, pp. 357 ff.
23. See Henry Mayer, *The New York Times*, October 27, 1946.
24. Kennedy, *op. cit.*, pp. 15–19.
25. *Ibid.*, p. 18.
26. Bernstein and Lovell, "Are Coal Strikes National Emergencies?," *Industrial and Labor Relations Review*, 6 (April, 1953), 366–367.
27. Kennedy, *op. cit.*, p. 19.
28. Hearings on the Donnell Resolution, p. 392.
29. Slichter, *The Challenge of Industrial Relations*, pp. 164–165.
30. *Ibid.*, pp. 165–166.
31. Rosenfarb, *Freedom and the Administrative State*, p. 149.
32. See Roberts, *Seizure in Labor Disputes*, and Teller, "Government Seizure in Labor Disputes," *Harvard Law Review*, LX (September, 1947), 1017.
33. Teller, *op. cit.*, pp. 1017–1019.
34. Reply Brief of Appellants, United States Court of Appeals, *Brotherhood of Locomotive Engineers et al. v. United States of America*, April, 1949, pp. 17–34.
35. *The New York Times*, February 23, 1951.
36. Reply Brief of Appellants, *op. cit.*, pp. 18–25.
37. *The New York Times*, February 23, 1951.
38. Quoted in Reply Brief of Appellants, *op. cit.*, p. 29.
39. Teller, *op. cit.*, p. 1030.
40. Johnson, *Government Seizure and Labor Disputes*, p. 143.
41. *The New York Times*, February 10 and 20, 1951.

42. *The New York Times*, February 9, 1951.
43. For a colorful description of this episode see Coffin, *Missouri Compromise*, Chap. 22.
44. U.S. Cong., Senate Report No. 496, *Dispute Between the Railway Carriers and Four Operating Brotherhoods*, June 27, 1951, p. 13.
45. *Ibid.*, p. 14.
46. Committee print, undated, pp. 13–14. See reference to this report in *The New York Times*, June 15, 1951.
47. U.S. Cong., Senate Report No. 496, *op. cit.*, pp. 14–15.
48. *Ibid.*, p. 15.
49. *U.S. v. Pewee Coal Co.*, 341 U.S. 114 (1951).
50. Gerhart, "Strikes and Eminent Domain," *Journal of the American Judicature Society*, XXX (December, 1946), 116.
51. Marceau and Musgrave, "Strikes in Essential Industries: A Way Out," *Harvard Business Review*, XXVII (May, 1949), 286. See also Goble, "The Nonstoppage Strike," *Labor Law Journal*, II (February, 1951), 105.
52. Marceau and Musgrave, *op. cit.*, pp. 287–292.
53. Hearings on the Donnell Resolution, p. 397.
54. U.S. Cong., Senate, *Labor Relations*, p. 294.
55. Davis, "Collective Bargaining and Economic Progress," in *Industrial Disputes and the Public Interest*, p. 14.
56. 61 *U.S. Statutes at Large*, 80th Cong., 1st Sess., Part I, Ch. 120, 136.
57. Millis and Brown, *From the Wagner Act to Taft-Hartley*, pp. 584–586.
58. *Ibid.*, p. 576.
59. Davis, *op. cit.*, p. 15.
60. Leiserson, "The Role of Government in Industrial Relations," *Industrial Disputes and the Public Interest*, p. 51.
61. *Ibid.*

XIV: SUMMARY

1. Clark, *Alternative to Serfdom*, p. 118.

BIBLIOGRAPHY

Books

Association of American Railroads. *A Review of Railway Operations in 1951*. Special Series # 84. Washington, 1952.

——— *Railroad Transportation, A Statistical Record, 1911–1949*. Washington, November, 1950.

Bakke, E. Wight, and Kerr, Clark. *Unions, Management, and the Public*. New York: Harcourt, Brace and Company, 1949.

Barger, Harold. *The Transportation Industry, 1889–1946*. New York: National Bureau of Economic Research, Inc., 1951.

Berman, Edward. *Labor Disputes and the President*. New York: Columbia University Press, 1924.

Bloom, Gordon F., and Northrup, Herbert R. *Economics of Labor and Industrial Relations*. Philadelphia: The Blakiston Company, 1950.

Bonavia, Michael R. *The Economics of Transport*. New Edition. London: Nisbet and Company, Ltd., 1947.

Chamberlain, Neil. *Collective Bargaining*. New York: McGraw-Hill Book Co., Inc., 1951.

Clark, John Maurice. *Alternative to Serfdom*. New York: Alfred A. Knopf, 1948.

Coffin, Tris. *Missouri Compromise*. Boston: Little, Brown and Company, 1947.

Commons, John A., and Andrews, John B. *Principles of Labor Legislation*. New York and London: Harper and Brothers, Inc., 1920.

Dale, Ernest. *Source of Economic Information for Collective Bargaining*. Research Report No. 17. New York: American Management Association, 1951.

Davis, William H. "Collective Bargaining and Economic Progress," *Industrial Disputes and the Public Interest.* Industrial Relations Institute, University of California, 1947.

Dearing, Charles L., and Owen, Wilford. *National Transportation Policy.* Washington: The Brookings Institution, 1949.

Ellis, Howard. "Economic Expansion Through Competitive Markets," in *Financing American Prosperity.* The Twentieth Century Fund, Inc., 1945.

Fabricant, Solomon. *Labor Savings in American Industry, 1899–1939.* Occasional Paper 23. National Bureau of Economic Research, Inc., November, 1945.

Fisher, Thomas Russell. *Industrial Disputes and Federal Legislation.* New York: Columbia University Press, 1940.

France, Robert R., and Lester, Richard A. *Compulsory Arbitration of Utility Disputes in New Jersey and Pennsylvania.* Princeton, N.J.; Industrial Relations Section, Department of Economics and Social Institutions, 1951.

Hansen, Alvin H. "Perspectives in Wage-Price Problems," in *Wage, Prices, and the National Welfare.* Institute of Industrial Relations, University of California, 1948.

——— "Stability and Expansion," in *Financing American Prosperity*, The Twentieth Century Fund, Inc., 1945.

Harris, Herbert. *American Labor.* New Haven: Yale University Press, 1938.

Hultgren, Thor. *American Transportation in Prosperity and Depression.* National Bureau of Economic Research, Inc., 1948.

Johnson, Richard Barney. *Government Seizure and Labor Disputes.* Philadelphia, 1948.

Jones, Harry E. (ed.). *Inquiry of the Attorney General's Committee on Administrative Procedure and Historical Background and Growth of Machinery Set-up for the Handling of Railroad Disputes, 1888–1940.* New York: Eastern Printing Corp., n.d.

Kaltenborn, Howard V. *Governmental Adjustment of Labor Disputes.* Chicago: Foundation Press, 1943.

Kirkland, Edward Chase. *Men, Cities, and Transportation.* Vol. II. Cambridge, Massachusetts: Harvard University Press, 1948.

Leiserson, William M. "The Role of Government in Industrial Relations," *Industrial Disputes and the Public Interest.* Industrial Relations Institute, University of California, 1947.

Lindsey, Almont. *The Pullman Strike*. Chicago: The University of Chicago Press, 1942.
Locklin, D. Philip. *Economics of Transportation*. 3rd ed. Chicago: Richard D. Irwin, Inc., 1947.
Loomis, Daniel F. *Railway Labor Legislation*. Washington: Association of American Railroads, 1950.
MacDonald, Lois. "Compulsory Arbitration in New Jersey," *Second Annual Conference on Labor*. New York: New York University, 1949.
Marshall, Alfred. *Principles of Economics*. 8th ed. New York: Macmillan and Company.
Metz, Harold W. *Labor Policy of the Federal Government*. Washington: The Brookings Institution, 1945.
Millis, Harry A., and Brown, Emily Clark. *From the Wagner Act to Taft-Hartley*. Chicago: The University of Chicago Press, 1950.
Millis, Harry A., and Montgomery, Royal A. *Organized Labor*. New York: McGraw-Hill Book Company, 1945.
Mills, F. C. *Prices in Recession and Recovery*. New York: National Bureau of Economic Research, Inc., 1936.
Monroe, J. Elmer. *Railroad Men and Wages*. Washington, 1947.
Moulton, Harold G., and Associates. *The American Transportation Problem*. Washington: The Brookings Institution, 1933.
National Industrial Conference Board. *The Economic Almanac for 1950*. New York, 1950.
Northrup, Herbert R., and Brinberg, Herbert R. *Economics of the Work Week*. National Industrial Conference Board, 1950.
Peterson, Florence. *American Labor Unions*. New York and London: Harper and Brothers, Inc., 1945.
Roberts, Harold S. *Seizure in Labor Disputes*. Honolulu: University of Hawaii, November, 1949.
Roe, Wellington. *Juggernaut*. Philadelphia: J. B. Lippincott Company, 1948.
Rosenfarb, Joseph. *Freedom and the Administrative State*. New York: Harper and Brothers, Inc., 1948.
Ross, Arthur M. *Trade Union Wage Policy*. Berkeley and Los Angeles: University of California Press, 1948.

Slichter, Sumner H. *Basic Criteria Used in Wage Negotiations.* The Chicago Convention of Commerce and Industry, 1947.

——— *The Challenge of Industrial Relations.* New York: Cornell University Press, 1947.

——— *Union Policies and Industrial Management.* Washington: The Brookings Institution, 1941.

Spencer, William H. *The National Railroad Adjustment Board.* Chicago: The University of Chicago Press, 1938.

Stewart, Bryce M., and Couper, Walter J. *Fact-Finding in Industrial Disputes.* New York: Industrial Relations Counselors, Inc., 1946.

Taylor, George W. "Can Wages Be Left to Collective Bargaining," in *Wages, Prices, and the National Welfare.* Institute of Industrial Relations, University of California, 1948.

——— *Government Regulation of Industrial Relations.* New York: Prentice-Hall, Inc., 1948.

Twentieth Century Fund, Inc. *How Collective Bargaining Works.* New York, 1942.

——— *Labor and the Government.* New York and London: McGraw-Hill Book Company, Inc., 1935.

Whitney, A. F. *Railroad Rules and Wages Movement in United States, 1944–45–46.* Brotherhood of Railroad Trainmen, 1946.

Witte, Edwin E. *The Government in Labor Disputes.* New York and London: McGraw-Hill Book Company, Inc., 1932.

Wolf, Harry D. *The Railroad Labor Board.* Chicago: The University of Chicago Press, 1927.

Yellen, Samuel. *American Labor Struggles.* New York: Harcourt, Brace and Company, 1936.

Articles

Bernstein, Irving, and Lovell, Hugh. "Are Coal Strikes National Emergencies?," *Industrial and Labor Relations' Review*, 6 (April, 1953).

Beyer, Otto S. "The Railway Labor Act," *Proceedings of the Academy of Political Science*, XXII, No. 1 (1946–1948).

Cottrell, W. F. "Death by Dieselization: A Case Study in the Reaction to Technological Change," *American Sociological Review*, XVI (June, 1951).

Dunlop, John T. "Fact-Finding in Labor Disputes," *Proceedings of the Academy of Political Science*, XXII, No. 1 (1946–1948).
——— "The Economics of Wage-Dispute Settlement," *Law and Contemporary Problems, Labor Dispute Settlement*, XII, No. 2, Duke University (Spring, 1947).
Ellingwood, A. R. "The Railway Labor Act of 1926," *Journal of Political Economy*, XXXVI (February, 1928).
Fabricant, Solomon. "Of Productivity Statistics: An Admonition," *Review of Economics and Statistics*, XXXI (November, 1949).
Fisher, Clyde O. "The New Railway Labor Act: A Comparison and Appraisal," *American Economic Review*, XVII (March, 1927).
Garrison, Lloyd K. "Labor Relations in the Railroad Industry," *Proceedings of the Academy of Political Science*, XVII (1936–1938).
——— "The National Railroad Adjustment Board: A Unique Administrative Agency," *Yale Law Journal*, XLVI (February, 1937).
Gerhart, Eugene L. "Strikes and Eminent Domain," *Journal of the American Judicature Society*, XXX (December, 1946).
Goble, George W. "The Nonstoppage Strike," *Labor Law Journal*, II, No. 2 (February, 1951).
Kaufman, Jacob J. "The Wage-Price Relationships in the Railroad Industry: A Comment," *Journal of Business*, XXVI (January, 1953).
——— "Wage Criteria in the Railroad Industry," *Industrial and Labor Relations Review*, 6 (October, 1952).
Kennedy, Thomas. "The Handling of Emergency Disputes," Industrial Relations Research Association, *Proceedings of Second Annual Meeting*, 1949.
Kerr, Clark. "The Short-Run Behavior of Physical Productivity and Average Hourly Earnings," *Review of Economics and Statistics*, XXXI (November, 1949).
Marceau, LeRoy, and Musgrave, Richard A. "Strikes in Essential Industries: A Way Out," *Harvard Business Review*, XXVII (May, 1949).
Meyers, Frederic, "Criteria in the Making of Wage Decisions by

'Neutrals': The Railroads as a Case Study," *Industrial and Labor Relations Review*, 4 (April, 1951).

Northrup, Herbert R. "A Critique of Pending Labor Legislation," *Political Science Quarterly*, LXI (June, 1946).

―――― "Emergency Disputes Under the Railway Labor Act," *Proceedings of First Annual Meeting*, Industrial Relations Research Association, 1948.

―――― "The Appropriate Bargaining Unit Question Under the Railway Labor Act," *Quarterly Journal of Economics*, LX (February, 1946).

―――― "The Railway Labor Act and Railway Labor Disputes in Wartime," *American Economic Review*, XXXVI (June, 1946).

―――― "Unfair Labor Practice Prevention Under the Railway Labor Act," *Industrial and Labor Relations Review*, III.

"Railroad Labor Disputes and the National Railroad Adjustment Board," *University of Chicago Law Review*, XVIII, No. 2 (Winter, 1951).

Reder, Melvin W. "The Significance of the 1948 General Motors Agreement," *Review of Economics and Statistics*, XXXI (February, 1949).

Roberts, Harold S. "Compulsory Arbitration of Labor Disputes in Public Utilities," *Labor Law Journal*, I (June, 1950).

Ross, Arthur M. "The General Motors Wage Agreement of 1948," *The Review of Economics and Statistics*, XXXI (February, 1949).

Shishkin, Boris. "The Case Against Compulsory Arbitration," *American Federatorist*, February, 1947.

Slichter, Sumner H. "The Great Question in Industrial Relations," *The New York Times Magazine*, April 27, 1947.

Taylor, George W. "Is Compulsory Arbitration Inevitable?," Industrial Relations Research Association, *Proceedings of First Annual Meeting*, 1948.

Teller, Ludwig. "Government Seizure in Labor Disputes," *Harvard Law Review*, LX (September, 1947).

Williams, Ernest W. "An Evaluation of Public Policy Toward the Railway Industry," *American Economic Review, Papers and Proceedings*, XLI (May, 1951).

Government Publications

Attorney-General's Committee on Administrative Procedure. *Railway Labor*, Monograph No. 17, Department of Justice. Washington, 1940.

Economic Report of the President, The. Transmitted to the Congress, January, 1953. Washington, 1953.

Federal Coordinator of Transportation. *A Survey of the Rules Governing the Wage Payments in Railroad Train and Engine Service*, Vol. I. Washington, March, 1936.

Hearings on Donnell Resolution. See U.S. Congress, Senate, *To Prohibit Strikes and to Provide for Compulsory Arbitration in the Railroad Industry*.

Hearings on Railroad Labor Dispute. See U.S. Congress, Senate, *Labor Dispute Between Railroad Carriers and Four Operating Brotherhoods*.

I.C.C. Statement No. M-300. See Interstate Commerce Commission, Bureau of Transport Economics and Statistics, *Wage Statistics of Class I Steam Railways in the United States*.

Interstate Commerce Commission. *Statistics of Railways in the United States, 1948*. Washington, 1950.

——— *Statistics of Railways in the United States, 1950*. Washington, 1952.

Interstate Commerce Commission, Bureau of Transport Economics and Statistics, *Factors in the Determination of Reasonable Levels of Fares for Motor Carriers of Passengers*. Docket # MC-C-550, Investigation of Bus Fares, November, 1948, Exhibit # 918, Witness: Fetter. (Mimeographed)

——— *Monthly Comment on Transportation Statistics*, August 13, 1948; February 15, 1950; July 13, 1950; February 18, 1951; April 13, 1951; July 13, 1951; January 14, 1953.

——— *Revenue Traffic Statistics of Class I Steam Railways in the United States*. Statement No. M-220, January through October, 1952.

——— *Wage Statistics of Class I Steam Railways in the United States*. Statements No. M-300.

——— *Yard Service Performance of Class I Steam Railways in the United States*, Statement No. M-215, December, 1950.

First Annual Report of the National Mediation Board, For the Fiscal Year Ended June 30, 1935.
Sixth Annual Report of the National Mediation Board, For the Fiscal Year Ended June 30, 1939.
Tenth Annual Report of the National Mediation Board, For the Fiscal Year Ended June 30, 1944.
Eleventh Annual Report of the National Mediation Board, For the Fiscal Year Ended June 30, 1948.
Fourteenth Annual Report of the National Mediation Board, For the Fiscal Year Ended June 30, 1948.
Sixteenth Annual Report of the National Mediation Board, For the Fiscal Year Ended June 30, 1950.
Seventeenth Annual Report of the National Mediation Board, For the Fiscal Year Ended June 30, 1951.
Eighteenth Annual Report of the National Mediation Board, For the Fiscal Year Ended June 30, 1952.
Office of Economic Stabilization. *Report of the President's Committee on the Cost of Living*, 1945.
U.S. Congress, Senate. *Dispute Between the Railway Carriers and Four Operating Brotherhoods*. Senate Report 496. 82nd Cong., 1st Sess., June 27, 1951.

——— *Labor Relations Program*. Hearings Before Committee on Labor and Public Welfare, on S.55 and S. J. Res. 22, Part 11. 80th Cong., 1st Sess.

——— *Labor Relations*. Hearings Before Committee on Labor and Public Welfare, on S.249, 1949. 81st Cong., 1st Sess.

——— *Labor Dispute Between Railroad Carriers and Four Operating Brotherhoods*. Hearings Before Committee on Labor and Public Welfare, February 22 to April 5, 1951. 82nd Cong., 1st Sess.

——— *To Prohibit Strikes and To Provide for Compulsory Arbitration in the Railroad Industry*. Hearings Before the Subcommittee on Railway Labor Act Amendments of the Committee on Labor and Public Welfare, May 8 to July 3, 1950. 81st Cong., 2nd Sess.

U.S. Department of Commerce and Labor. "Mediation and Arbitration of Railway Labor Disputes in the United States, by

Charles P. Neill, *Bulletin of the Bureau of Labor*, No. 98, January, 1912.

U.S. Department of Labor. *The Termination Report, National War Labor Board*, Vol. I. Washington, 1948.

U.S. Department of Labor, Bureau of Labor Statistics. *Cost of Living Wage Adjustment in Collective Bargaining*, September, 1950.

——— *Federal Fact-Finding Boards of Inquiry*, n.d. (Mimeographed)

——— *Hours and Earnings*, February, 1953.

——— *Techniques of Preparing Major BLS Statistical Series*, Bulletin No. 993, 1950.

——— *Use of Federal Power in Settlement of Railway Labor Disputes*, by Clyde Olin Fisher, Bulletin No. 303, March, 1922.

——— *Monthly Labor Review*, November, 1942; August, 1946; July, 1947; June, 1948.

——— *Monthly Labor Review*, July, 1948. "Cost of Living Wage Clauses and the UAW-GM Pact."

——— *Monthly Labor Review*, August, 1948.

——— *Monthly Labor Review*, January, 1951. "Analysis of Strikes, 1927–1949."

——— *Monthly Labor Review*, March, 1951; May, 1951; January, 1953, March, 1953.

Arbitration, Emergency, and Adjustment Board Reports and Awards

Boards of Arbitration, National Mediation Board. Docket # A-2215, Arb. 61 and 62, 2 Labor Arbitration Reports 251, 286.

Board of Arbitration, NMB Case A-2595, Arbitration 91, Award, September 2, 1947, 8 Labor Arbitration Reports 204.

National Railroad Adjustment Board, First Division. *Awards*. LaGrange, Illinois: Suburban Printers and Publishers.

N.R.A.B. Award. See National Railroad Adjustment Board, First Division. *Awards*.

Referee's Decision and Award, *In the Matter of a Controversy Between Brotherhood of Railroad Trainmen and Certain Par-*

ticipating *Eastern, Western, and Southeastern Railroads of the United States*, August 7, 1951.

Report of the Board of Arbitration in Matter of Controversy Between the Eastern Railroads and the Brotherhood of Locomotive Engineers, November 2, 1912.

Report to the President by the Emergency Board, October 29, 1938; November 5, 1941; May 24, 1943; September 25, 1943; April 18, 1946; March 27, 1948; December 17, 1948; April 29, 1949; September 19, 1949; April 18, 1950; June 15, 1950; January 25, 1952.

Supplementary Report to the President by the Emergency Board, May 29, 1943.

Supplementary Report to the President by the Emergency Board, Mediation Settlement, December 5, 1941.

LEGISLATION

Kansas Laws, Special Session, 1920, c. 29.

Public Law 914, Ch. 1220. 81st Congress, 2nd Session.

25 *U.S. Statutes at Large* 501, Ch. 1063. 50th Congress, 1st Session.

30 *U.S. Statutes at Large* 424, Ch. 370. 55th Congress, 2nd Session.

38 *U.S. Statutes at Large* 103, Ch. 6. 63rd Congress, 1st Session.

39 *U.S. Statutes at Large* 643, Ch. 48. 64th Congress, 1st Session, Part I.

39 *U.S. Statutes at Large* 721, Ch. 436. 64th Congress, 1st Session, Part I.

41 *U.S. Statutes at Large* 456, Ch. 91. 66th Congress, 2nd Session, Part I.

44 *U.S. Statutes at Large* 577, Ch. 347. 69th Congress, 1st Session, Part II.

47 *U. S. Statutes at Large* 1467, Ch. 204. 72nd Congress, 2nd Session.

48 *U.S. Statutes at Large* 211, Ch. 91. 73rd Congress, 1st Session.

48 *U.S. Statutes at Large* 1185, Ch. 691. 73rd Congress, 2nd Session.

50 *U.S. Statutes at Large* 307, Ch. 382. 75th Congress, 1st Session, Part I.

54 U.S. Statutes at Large 898, Ch. 722. 76th Congress, 3rd Session, Part I.
54 U.S. Statutes at Large 906, Ch. 722. 76th Congress, 3rd Session, Part I.
61 U.S. Statutes at Large 136, Ch. 120. 80th Congress, 1st Session, Part I.

CASES

Adair v. United States, 208 U.S. 161 (1908).
Bluefield Waterworks Co. v. Public Service Commission, 262 U.S. 679 (1923).
Clements et al. v. United States, 266 U.S. 605 (1924).
Dorchy v. Kansas, 272 U.S. 306 (1926).
Order of Railway Conductors v. Southern Railroad Co., 339 U.S. 255 (1950).
Pennsylvania Railroad Co. v. U.S. Railroad Labor Board et al., 261 U.S. 72 (1922).
Slocum v. Delaware, Lackawanna, and Western Railway Company, 339 U.S. 239 (1950).
Texas and New Orleans, Railroad Company et al. v. Brotherhood of Railway and Steamship Clerks et al., 281 U.S. 548 (1930).
United Auto Workers v. Wisconsin Employment Relations Board, 336 U.S. 245 (1949).
United States v. Brotherhood of Locomotive Engineers et al., 79 Federal Supplement 485 (1948).
United States v. Brotherhood of Railroad Trainmen et al., 95 Federal Supplement 1019 (1951).
United States v. Pewee Coal Co., 341 U.S. 114 (1951).
United States v. United Mine Workers, 330 U.S. 258 (1947).
1 War Labor Reports 325, The Bureau of National Affairs.
9 War Labor Reports xii–xv. The Bureau of National Affairs.
Wilson v. New, 243 U.S. 332 (1916).
Wolff Packing Company v. Court of Industrial Relations, 262 U.S. 522 (1923) and 267 U.S. 552 (1925).
Youngstown Sheet and Tube Co., et al. v. Charles Sawyer, decided June 2, 1952.

Miscellaneous

Brief for Appellee, United States of America, U.S. Court of Appeals, District of Columbia, *Brotherhood of Locomotive Engineers et al., United States of America.*

Carriers Exhibit No. 37, *Productivity of the Railroad Industry*, presented to the Emergency Board (# 81), Appointed by the President on February 24, 1950.

Carriers Exhibit No. 38, *Financial Condition of the Railroads*, presented to the Emergency Board, Appointed by the President on February 24, 1950.

Ex Parte No. 148, 248 I.C.C. 545 (1942).

Ex Parte No. 162, 276 I.C.C. 9 (1949).

Ex Parte No. 175, August 8, 1951 and April 11, 1952.

Federal Register, Vol. 11, Nos. 34 and 49.

General Regulation No. 8, of the Economic Stabilization Administrator, issued March, 1951, revised August 23, 1951, and amended effective December 7, 1951.

General Wage and Rule Agreements, Decisions, Awards and Orders, Governing Employees Engaged in Engine Service on Railroads in the United States, 1907–1941, and Vol. II, 1942–1948, The Brotherhood of Locomotive Firemen and Enginemen, Cleveland, Ohio.

Issues Before the Emergency Board and the Closing Argument for the Carriers in the Engineers' and Trainmen's 1946 Rules Case. Eastern, Western, and Southeastern Carriers' Conference Committees, 1946.

Letter, General Chairman of Grievance Committee, Brotherhood of Locomotive Firemen, and Enginemen, New York Central Lines, West, August 7, 1951.

1946 Transcript. See *Transcript of Proceedings of Emergency Board*, Chicago, Illinois, 1946.

1948 Transcript. See *Transcript of Proceedings of Emergency Board*, Chicago, Illinois, 1948.

Referee's Memorandum and Award, March 18, 1953.

Reply Brief of Appellants, United States Court of Appeals, *Brotherhood of Locomotives Engineers et al. v. United States of America*, April, 1949.

Report Covering the Wage Movement of 1943, issued by the Brotherhood of Locomotive Firemen and Enginemen, Order of Railway Conductors, and the Switchmen's Union of North America, n.d.

Report to the President of the United States on the Labor Dispute in the Basic Steel Industry, September 10, 1949, 3 American Labor Arbitration Awards, 68, 318.

Transcript of Proceedings of the Emergency Board, Chicago, Illinois, 1946. New York: Eastern Printing Corp., n.d.

Transcript of Proceedings of the Emergency Board, Chicago, Illinois, 1948. New York: Eastern Printing Corp., n.d.

Transcript of Proceedings of Emergency Board, Chicago, Illinois, 1950. New York: Eastern Printing Corp., n.d.

U.S. Department of Labor, *Report and Recommendations of the Fact-Finding Board . . . in the Dispute Between the Milwaukee Gas Light Co. and Local 18, United Gas, Coke, and Chemical Workers of America (C.I.O.), September 14, 1946*, 4 Labor Arbitration Reports 537.

INDEX

Act of August 29, 1916, 128-129
Adair v. *United States*, 196
Adamson Act, of 1916, 28, 61; 62-63
Adjustment boards, 66; *see also* National Railroad Adjustment Board
Air hose coupling, 40, 41
American Train Dispatchers Association, 53
Arbitraries, 23, 35; *see also* Working rules
Arbitration, extent of, 82
Arbitration Act of 1888, 55-57
Arbitration award, 1953, productivity, 112
Arbitration board report, 1946, 104; 1947, 104
Assignment of work, 33

Bankruptcy Act of 1933, amendments to, 69
Bluefield Waterworks Co. v. *Public Service Commission*, 7
Board of Mediation, 66
Board of Railroad Wages and Working Conditions, 29
Brotherhood of Locomotive Engineers, 46, 47, 50
Brotherhood of Locomotive Firemen and Enginemen, 46, 47, 50, 149
Brotherhood of Maintenance of Way Employees, 53
Brotherhood of Railroad Signalmen of America, 53
Brotherhood of Railroad Trainmen, 46, 47, 87, 88, 133, 149

Brotherhood of Railway and Steamship Clerks, *et al.*, 53
Brotherhood of Railway Carmen of America, 53

Check-off, 198
Clark, J. M., 186
Clark, Tom, 130-131
Clements et al. v. *U.S.*, 214
Closed shop, 71; *see also* Union shop
Commission of Eight, 28
Committee of the Council of National Defence, 28
Company-unions, 69, 71
Compulsion, *see* labor disputes
Compulsory arbitration, 164, 196; effects on collective bargaining, 164-165; in foreign countries, 166; effectiveness of, 166-167; in the U.S., 166-167
Consolidation of railroad facilities, 12
Constructive allowances, 23; *see also* Working rules
Consumer Price Index, 98
Conversion rule, 35, 40
Cost of living, changes in, 98; *see also* Wage criteria
Criteria for wage setting, *see* Wage criteria

Dieselization, 16
Director of Economic Stabilization, 85, 102-103
Dorchy v. *Kansas*, 214
Dual basis of wage payment, 22, 24

Earnings, *see* Wages
Economic stabilization, *see* Director of Economic Stabilization
Eight-hour work day, 28, 62-63
Emergency board report, 1936, 37, 99-100, 110, 115, 123; 1941, 37-38, 100-101, 110, 115-116, 123; 1943, 38, 102, 111-112, 116, 123, 125; 1946, 38, 104, 111, 116-117, 123-124; 1947, 105, 117-118; 1948, 38-39, 40, 105, 111, 118, 120, 124; 1950, 39-40, 40-41, 106, 111, 118-119, 120-121, 124; 1952, 194; *see also* Wage and rules movement
Emergency boards, wage standards of, 95-126; effectiveness of, 154-156; suggestions for improvements, 156; acceptance of decisions of, 156-157; recommendations of, 202; attitudes of parties toward, 202
Emergency Railroad Transportation Act, 13, 69
Employment, 4, 18 ff.; guarantee of, after consolidation, 13; changes in, by occupation, 20-21
Equipment, manning and use of, 34-35
Erdman Act of 1898, 28, 57-60, 66
Escalator clause, 106, 108
Essential industries, strikes in, 168-169

Fact-finding boards, effectiveness of, 155-156; *see also* Emergency boards
Federal Control of Railroads, 63; *see also* Government intervention; Seizure
Federal Coordinator of Transportation, 69
Forty-hour work week, *see* Wage criteria, maintenance of take-home pay with reduction in hours

Garrison, Lloyd K., 150
Government intervention, by courts, 60, 63, 87, 128 ff., 135; by President, 59, 60, 84 ff., 106, legal justification for, 128-129, effects of, 133-135
Green, William, 176
Grievance disputes, *see* National Railroad Adjustment Board
Grievances, principles for settlement of, 137-138; number of, 144; procedures, evaluation of, 140 ff., recommendations for improvement of, 148-149, suggestions for improvement of, 150-151, causes of breakdown of, 146 ff.; strikes over, 143-144; promptness in settlement of, 144; delays in settlement of, 147; refusal to accept awards, 148

Hose, coupling of, 33, 40, 41
Hotel and Restaurant Employees International Alliance, *et al.*, 53

Improvement factor, 112; *see also* Productivity
Injunctions, 87, 129; violations of, 172; *see also* Norris–La Guardia Act
Interdivisional runs, 32-33, 40, 41, 194
International Association of Machinists, 53
International Brotherhood of Blacksmiths, *et al.*, 53
International Brotherhood of Boilermakers, *et al.*, 53
International Brotherhood of Electrical Workers, 53
International Brotherhood of Firemen and Oilers, 53
International Longshoremen's Association, 53

INDEX

Interstate Commerce Act, 12-13, 56
Interstate Commerce Commission, 13 ff., 95, 121-122, 125; rates and rate-making procedure, 7, 9-10, 11-12
Intervention, by government, see Government intervention

Labor disputes, government intervention in, 55-73; compulsion in, 127-136; compulsory arbitration of, 127, 135; delays in settlements of, 157-159; complexity of issues in, 160-161
Labor organizations, 45-54; conflicts among, 50-52; see also Company-unions; Nonoperating Unions; Operating Unions
Little Steel Formula, 98, 102

Marshall, Alfred, 1
Mediation, 82-84; see also National Mediation Board
Mileage, limitations of, 23
Morse, Wayne L., 74, 168
Murphy, Frank, 130

National Marine Engineers' Beneficial Association, 53
National Mediation Board, 45, 71, 72, 74, 75, 79, 81, 127
National Organization of Masters, Mates, and Pilots of America, 53
National Railroad Adjustment Board, 3, 30, 31-35, 42, 72; organization of, 138-139; evaluation of operations of, 140 ff.; procedures of, 140; functions of, 141; attitude of railroads and labor toward, 141-42; avoidance of machinery of, 142-143; enforcement of decisions of, 143; number of cases, 145, 211
National Recovery Act, 120

Newlands Act of 1913, 28, 60-62, 66
Nonoperating unions, 45, 48, 52-53
Nonoperating workers, working rules, 27; wages of, 93
Norris–La Guardia Act, 129, 131, 171; see also Injunctions
Northrup, Herbert, 85
NRA, 120

Operating unions, 45, 48; strikes, 81
Operating workers, wages of, 93
Order of Railroad Telegraphers, 53
Order of Railway Conductors of America, 46, 47, 87
Order of Railway Conductors v. Southern Railway Co., 212
Overtime, 24, 34

Pennsylvania Railroad Co. v. U.S. Railroad Labor Board, 197
Perkins, Frances, 71, 74
Productivity, 93, 112; of railroad workers, 19, 113, 205; of manufacturing, changes in, 93; see also Wage criteria
Public utilities, strikes in, 167
Pullman strike, 57

Railroad industry, size and importance, 1, 4; background of, 4-17; net investment, 4; traffic, 4, 5, 9; number of Class I carriers, 5; financial condition of, 6; profits, standards, 7; profits of, 8; competition, 9; rate-making procedure, 9 (see also Interstate Commerce Commission); rates, rigidity of, 10; technology, 15-16; dieselization of, 16; capital expenditures of, 17; employment, 18, 19 (see also Employment); union organization, degree of, 45 (see also Unionism)

Railroad Labor Board, 66, 149
Railway Labor Executives Association, 47
Railroad Yardmasters of America, 53
Railroads, consolidation of facilities, 12
Railway Labor Act, 1926 Legislation, 66-69; amendments of 1934, 30, 69, 70, provisions of, 3, 70-71, 138-140, 163, effectiveness of, 71-72, 74-77, attitudes of parties toward, 140-141; amendments of 1952, 198; appraisal of, 78-89; evaluation of, 153-154; recommendations for improvement of, 185-186; defects in, 153-161
Rate of return, *see* Railroad industry profits; Wage criteria, ability to pay
Richberg, Donald, 163
Roosevelt, Franklin D., 134
Rules, *see* Working rules

Seizure, 2, 72, 81, 86, 87, 131, 164; legal justification for, 128-131; steel industry, 131; effects on collective bargaining, 165-166; meaning of, 170; effectiveness of, 170-171; legality of, 171-172; evaluation of, 172-173; equity of, 173-174; plans for, 174-175
Selective Service Act, 132
Senate Committee on Labor and Public Welfare, 1951 hearings and report, 72
Sheet Metal Workers International Association, 53
Slichter, Sumner, 26, 155
Slocum v. Delaware, Lackawanna, and Western Railroad Co., 212
Smith-Connally Act, 134
Special allowances, 35; *see also* Working rules

Starting time, rules for, 32
Steel Industry Board, report of, 114
Steelman, John R., 134
Strike, right to, 162-178
Strikes, 72, 143-144; effect of, 5-6; Pullman, 57; evaluation of data on, 78-82; number of, 78-79, 146; of operating unions, 81; threatened, 81; attitudes toward, 162; attitude of AF of L toward, 163-164; legality of, 164; in public utilities, 167; opposition to, 169 ff.; attitude of Congress toward, 176-177
Switching limits, 32, 40, 41, 194
Switchmen's Union of North America, 41, 46 f., 49 f., 87, 106, 131

Taft-Hartley Law, 130, 131-132, 176-177
Taft, Robert A., 177
Taylor, George W., 165
Transportation Act of 1920, 63-65; of 1940, 13, 47, 122
Truman, Harry S., 71, 135

Unionism, degree of, 45, 46, 53, 54; organizational conflicts, 50-52
Union shop, 198, 202; *see also* Closed shop
Unions, *see* Company-unions; Labor organizations; Nonoperating Unions; Operating Unions
United Auto Workers v. Wisconsin Employment Relations Board, 214
United Railroad Operating Crafts, 52, 195
United States Railroad Labor Board, 64-65
United States v. Brotherhood of Locomotive Engineers et al., 201, 209

INDEX

United States v. Brotherhood of Railroad Trainmen et al., 201
United States v. Pewee Coal Co., 216
United States v. Switchmen's Union of North America, 188
United States v. United Mine Workers, 129

Wage and rules movement, 1937, 37, 48, 84; 1038, 37, 48, 84, 98-100; 1941, 37, 49, 84, 100; 1942, 85-86, 102-103; 1943, 38, 49; 1945, 38, 49, 103; 1946, 86; 1947, 38-39, 86, 104; 1948, 87, 105; 1949, 39-40, 49-50, 87-88, 105; see also Emergency board report
Wage changes, attitude of railroads and labor toward, 92-93; criteria for, see Wage criteria
Wage criteria, difficulty of developing set of, 96; changes in cost of living, 98-109, attitude of railroads toward, 98-99, 100, attitude of labor toward, 99, 100, attitudes of emergency boards toward, 1926–1950, 99-106, economic implications of, 107-109; changes in productivity, 109-114; wages paid in other industries, 114-119; maintenance of take-home pay with reduction in hours, 120-121; ability to pay, 122-124; hazards of employment, 125; budget standards, 125; irregularity of employment, 125
Wage payments, methods of, 21 ff.
Wage Stabilization Board, 88
Wages, 4; methods of payment, 21-26; guarantees of, 24; of railroad workers, 80, 91, 93, 112-113, 205

Washington Job Protection Agreement, 13, 47
Wilson v. New, 197
Wolf, Harry D., 74
Wolff Packing Company v. Court of Industrial Relations, 214
Working rules, 26-43; development of, 26; reasons for, 26; nonoperating workers, 27; origin of, 27-31; description of, 31-35; effect of, 35; National Railroad Adjustment Board, interpretations of, 31-35; railroads' attitudes toward, 37; effect on collective bargaining, 41-43; effect on settlement of grievances, 146-147; attitudes of emergency boards toward, 194
——— types of: assignments, 31-32; yard service, 31; yard assignments, 31-32; operations, 31-33; full crew, 32; starting time, 32; switching limits, 32, 40, 41, 194; yard limits, 32, 40; interdivisional runs, 32, 33, 40, 41, 194; coupling hose, 33, 40, 41; assignments of work, 33-34; overtime, 34; use of equipment, 34; self-propelled equipment, 34; manning of equipment, 34; deadheading, 35; side trips, 35; special allowances, 35; arbitraries, 35; delays at terminal, 35; more than one class of service, 35; conversion, 35, 40; "8 within 9," 23, 191
Work shifts, 32
Work stoppages, see Strikes

Yard assignments, 31
Yard limits, 32, 40
"Yellow-dog" contract, 69